INTO HARM'S WAY

INTO HARM'S WAY

MY LIFE IN CORRECTIONS
—AND THE HISTORIC RIOT THAT NEARLY ENDED IT

By Richard A. Nelson
with Patti Sewall

PS Communications
ATTN: Permissions Coordinator
P.O. Box 739
Sloughhouse, CA. 95683

Publisher's Note: This book is a work of nonfiction. It is a memoir about historical events, and therefore is the author's version of events as he experienced them and as he remembers them.

All photographs are from the author's collection.
Book Layout and Design by The Book Makers LLC.
Editing by Susan Hart Snyder

INTO HARM'S WAY
My life in Corrections – and the historic riot that nearly ended it
By Richard A. Nelson with Patti Sewall -- 1st ed.

Trade Paperback ISBN 978-1-7339369-0-3
Hard Cover ISBN 978-1-7339369-1-0

"Dick Nelson will always be remembered as someone who saved multiple correctional officers' lives on August 21, 1971."

— *Captain Donald McGraw, San Quentin State Prison*

"I will never forget George Jackson pulling a gun from under a wig on his head. Within minutes, six people were dead. Lt. Dick Nelson saved our lives that fateful day."

— *Correctional Officer Urbano 'Rubi' Rubiaco,*
survivor of the 1971 riot at San Quentin

"Unfortunately for us, we had the weapons but we didn't have Dick Nelson at Attica. If we had, I'm certain the incident wouldn't have gone into darkness that first day."

— *Don Almeter, retired New York corrections officer*
and hostage survivor of the deadly riot at
Attica Correctional Facility in September 1971

"Dick Nelson is one of my heroes. Without regard for his own safety, and with other brave responding officers, the savage revolt was halted and lives were saved. Though nearly five decades have past, it is still hard to forget the horror endured and witnessed by the courageous officers who were there on August. 21, 1971. The selfless service of those men commands and deserves the respect and recognition of all of us whose lives are made safer by such courage."

— *Judge Terrence Boren, a Marin County prosecutor in the*
San Quentin Six trial in 1974, and in the 1985 case against
George Jackson's attorney Stephen Bingham

CONTENTS

FOREWORD

The socially turbulent decade of the 1960s quietly rolled in but it definitely stormed out. One of the most emotionally supercharged decades in American history, the '60s witnessed:

- The assassinations of President John F. Kennedy, Senator Robert Kennedy, and Martin Luther King Jr.
- The first heart transplant, the first Super Bowl, and the first murder by the Zodiac killer
- The Baby Boomers' entrance into college, the Beatles arriving in America, and the Eagle landing on the moon
- The war raging in Vietnam, and the Civil Rights advocates marching in our neighborhoods

Of all those remarkable events, the Civil Rights movement generated an extraordinary amount of attention. It united a diverse group of Americans, from our universities to the political arena, and from the Hollywood elite to those living in our poorest areas. Freedom was the common battle cry of citizens who rose up in unison.

Unfortunately, a growing contingent of violent revolutionaries and their supporters, who replaced cries for equality with demands that drew blood, ultimately overshadowed the more peaceful efforts of others in the crusade.

And when the late 60s erupted into the early 70s, the tsunami of this radicalized counterculture washed up over the walls of California's San Quentin State Prison.

There have been many books and articles written over the years about the historic incident that took place at San Quentin in August 1971, as radical, vengeful prisoners answered the call to revolt. Some of those stories have been told mainly through the eyes of the one man who ignited the firestorm – revolutionary inmate George Jackson. Nelson's story is different.

Within these pages, Nelson fills in the chapter that's been missing from so many accounts of that horrific day. And along the way he gives readers a rare glimpse behind the wall, past bumbling crooks and escape artists, into a max-security cell block, and inside the minds of career criminals and violent sociopaths. But Nelson's book is more than a riveting memoir.

Into Harm's Way is an American true crime story about the definitive risks that come with working in a prison. It unveils portraits of bravery beyond belief in the midst of man's inhumanity to man. More important, it's a story about having the courage and character to do the right thing at the right time.

The hard-charging military leader General George S. Patton observed that all men are afraid in battle. "The coward is the one who lets his fear overcome his sense of duty."

Nelson exemplifies the integrity and dedication it takes to maintain the security of America's correctional institutions, especially in the face of sudden violence. His actions on that dark Saturday in 1971 should be the standard for the profession. It was a defining moment in leadership by example.

As law enforcement groups across the nation struggle with repurposed prejudices that never really went away, and the violence that typically accompanies them, correctional peace officers know it's only a matter of time before the wave of revolt spills over into America's prisons – again.

Do our correctional facilities still employ heroes like Dick Nelson? Let's hope so.

Retired Correctional Lieutenant Don Novey,
thirty-one years in Corrections;
respected public safety advocate since 1968

INTRODUCTION

SUNDAY AUGUST 1, 1971

The Visitor Center at San Quentin State Prison was naturally busy on Sundays, the day reserved for family visits. Inmate attorneys and their legal assistants were not allowed to visit on Sundays. So instead of grim-faced men in suits carrying briefcases and talking in low tones, the waiting room was busy with the chatter of children, young wives, and long-suffering mothers so burdened with disappointment you could read it on their faces.

The large room was not air-conditioned, and August in Marin County could be unusually warm with little fog off the Bay to cool the air. A worn, U-shaped wooden table with matching benches sat in the middle of the room. It served as the visiting area for the general population inmates – those at little risk for trouble. San Quentin's higher-risk inmates, especially those I supervised in the Adjustment Center, would take their visits in one of two private cubicles behind closed doors. The small rooms included a couple of chairs, and a wooden table with a moveable, steel mesh grate that could be lowered into place to separate inmate from visitor. This went a long way toward discouraging violent outbursts and contraband smuggling.

In the warm waiting area, adult visitors fanned themselves with magazines, smoked cigarette after cigarette, and drank *Coca-Cola* from cans out of the vending machine. Glass soda bottles were not allowed in any area where inmates might come in contact with them. Thick shards of broken glass make excellent deadly weapons. As they waited for their visits, frustrated parents used small toys and coloring books to keep their little ones amused.

Correctional officers working the check-in desk had their hands full making sure all visitors were on the inmates' approved lists, and both visitors and inmates followed the rules. No handbags or other personal items were allowed in the visiting areas. And visits were kept chaste to make sure no drugs made their way past ruby red lips and into an inmate's body via a passionate kiss from a visitor.

If you didn't have a headache before your shift started, a weekend assignment in the crowded, noisy Visitor Center could give you one. Five correctional officers were assigned to handle the visiting process: one at the inmate check-in desk, two to supervise the general population visiting area, a search officer between the front count gate and the visiting area, and one as an observer in the hallway behind the two secure cubicles. Here, the observing officer would periodically look through the small windows on the cubicle doors to ensure high-risk inmates and their visitors were behaving. It was largely efficient for the times, though not foolproof.

In the midst of the widespread civil unrest of that era, my staff and I did our best to stay focused on the tasks at hand as we batted away haunting premonitions of inmate uprisings like they were flies on a steaming pile of horse manure. In the months leading up to the summer of 1971, the tension was as thick as swamp mud in that prison. Staff assaults and other violent incidents were on the rise. Recent killings at Soledad Prison and San Quentin added to the menacing atmosphere. A heavy cloud of uncertainty hovered over the facility and refused to dissipate. As if we needed one more glaring red flag of trouble on the horizon, the universe reached out and gave us a doozy.

◆

Two women and their children arrived to check in for an inmate visit. They had been here before and were no strangers to the process. As was policy, they were instructed to walk through the metal-detecting Inspectoscope Gate – a device intended to eliminate the possibility of weapons being smuggled into the prison.

There is hardly a worse scenario in the prison business than an inmate armed with a gun and ammunition, thanks to a visitor just as criminally motivated as the inmate behind bars. It is the most devious of plots as it puts an entire institution and the surrounding community in danger all at once.

The women walked through the metal detector without incident. Then the children were asked to do so. As one young boy walked through, the machine's alarm beeped out its warning. He was asked to walk through again, and again the alarm went off. The officer manning the area asked the boy to remove his shoes before walking through once more, thinking the buckles might be the culprit. Still, the alarm responded to some unknown metal object. A closer inspection by the officer revealed that someone had taped a fake pistol to the boy's lower leg, concealing it under his pants.

The two women were the sisters of inmate George Jackson – a known Black Panther extremist awaiting trial for the murder of a correctional officer. The brazen attempt to see if a pistol could be smuggled into the visiting area was enough to deny Jackson's sisters any visitation for an indefinite period of time. It was also an obvious clue to an escape plan that should have put San Quentin on high alert. It didn't.

Surprisingly, prison authorities didn't react as strongly as they should have to this serious infraction. In fact, I wasn't even told about the attempted smuggling. As the supervising lieutenant in the Adjustment Center, also known as the Lockup, I should have been immediately informed so I could direct my staff to be especially vigilant for suspicious behavior on the part of the dangerous inmates housed there. Certainly, we would have paid closer attention to the activities of George Jackson.

Had my staff and I been officially notified, we may have been able to prevent the tragedy that occurred in the Lockup just three weeks later.

SATURDAY AUGUST 21, 1971

I'd really rather be fishing today, I grumbled mostly to myself, though my seven-year-old daughter was standing beside me in our dining room. Jill was tall and thin, and her blonde hair as a toddler had turned a light brown to match her eyes. She resembled my side of the family and was definitely a daddy's girl. Nothing pleased her more than shadowing me on the weekends as I tended to projects around the house. As Jill fiddled with the paint cans and brushes in the corner of the room, I started the grunt work of taping off the windows and doorframes in preparation for a Saturday painting session.

It was a warm, sunny afternoon, and house painting was definitely not my preferred activity for a day off work. Typically, without the restrictions of my wife's honey-do list, I'd load up my tackle box and spend a few hours fishing the choppy, sapphire-blue waters of the San Francisco Bay.

As a correctional lieutenant at San Quentin State Prison in Marin County, I had the opportunity to live on the grounds of the 160-year-old facility that stands like a Middle Ages citadel on the Bay's rocky shoreline. San Quentin's medieval-looking, three-story cell blocks, constructed in the early 1850s, stand in stark contrast to the more architecturally modern and beautifully restored buildings just about twenty miles to the south in San Francisco. Somewhere between those contrasting images, we found our Victorian dream home in officer's housing on the grounds of San Quentin.

With the skyline of the world-famous city as a backdrop, Marin County is a beautiful boatride just across the Bay from San Francisco. More important, the region is a diehard fisherman's paradise – and I am a diehard fisherman.

The unavoidable stress of prison work is no match for a day out on the Bay. The beautiful California coastline, the aromatic spray of the Pacific Ocean, and the occasional glimpse of oceanic creatures large and small is a 180-degree relaxation swing from the pressure of running two maximum security housing units. Whether I was out on the open sea casting for salmon, fishing for perch off the Marin Pier with my kids, or trolling for striped bass out in the Bay, the calm discipline of the sport of fishing is a far cry from keeping the peace in a cell block full of California's most dangerous felons.

A prison environment is a unique collection of law breakers of varying personalities and levels of behavior, all living together behind razor-wire-topped fences and thirty-foot-tall granite walls. The job duties of a correctional peace officer are far more complex than simply watching convicts age in their cells, a myth I'm sure some people still believe. And supervising the high-profile felons in a maximum security cell block is an adventure all its own.

All max-custody inmates should be considered dangerous, but some are downright evil – society's worst beings. They're deviant violent sociopaths, ruthless gang members, hateful cop killers, and predators of all shapes, sizes, and felonious obsessions. And they all believe the rules of society – and sometimes the rules in prison – don't apply to them.

For me, a day spent in quiet solitude on the Pacific Ocean definitely helps to cleanse the rude stench of incarceration from my senses. And considering our location in the lap of one of the nation's busiest cities, I was also grateful every day for my short and uneventful work commute.

Those poor suckers, I often muttered as I watched the southbound traffic on Highway 101 back up like ants bumper-to-bumper on a picnic table. I'd shake my head as I imagined the frustrating morning and evening rituals that so many in San

Francisco's workforce participated in five days a week. No thank you. I'd take a day shift in a crowded Lockup over that any day.

◆

Our roomy old Victorian home sat on a hill overlooking San Quentin's main entrance, giving a birds-eye view into the large main yard of the prison. At a generous 3,600 square feet, featuring five bedrooms, it was ideal for our growing family of three daughters and one son, all under the age of thirteen. It was a perfect fit for our family, and even though a big house meant big upkeep, my wife, Shirley, and I fell in love with it at first sight.

Grudgingly, I finished the prep work in the old dining room that had seen its fair share of paint and wallpaper over the years, keeping a positive outlook by thinking about the couple of wine coolers chilling in the fridge. I never was a hard-liquor kind of guy, and beer was my cheap, social beverage in my college days. Once married, my taste buds drifted over to wine coolers and spritzers, especially in the summertime.

That'll be my reward for a job well done, I thought with a bit of resentment over my wife's determination to spruce up the house before the holidays rounded the corner. Unfortunately, I had to wait much longer than I anticipated to collect that reward. My painting project was abruptly halted by the piercing sound of a gunshot.

Normally, I enjoy the faint sound of gunfire from the rifle range during training sessions, along with the accompanying odor of cordite wafting across my prison valley. After all, I'm an outdoorsman and a law enforcement officer. But this incident was entirely different, and the gunshot didn't come from the range. On the grounds of a state prison, the sudden sound of close gunfire is enough to rattle your soul. It's a force that splits the air like thunder.

I was outside taking a break from the paint fumes when I heard it. Immediately, I ran around to the front of the house where I'd have a better view down into the prison. The gunfire had definitely come from inside the prison walls, but exactly where and why? And just then it hit me. As sure as I was of my own name I knew at that moment what was happening. I'd been dreading this incident for some time. Whatever violence was taking place inside those walls, I was certain who was at the center of it. And I knew he must be stopped at all costs.

In that instant, as my mind raced and my lungs refused to exhale, a wave came over me. I realized that everything I had learned about keeping the peace behind prison walls would be tested before the sun went down.

That Saturday in August 1971 turned out to be one of the deadliest and most defining days in the history of Corrections in California —a dark distinction it still holds today. But I'm getting ahead of myself. My story actually begins in Foxhome, Minnesota.

CHAPTER ONE

ROAD TO THE BIG HOUSE

"Life can only be understood backwards,
but it must be lived forwards."
—Soren Kierkegaard

When I was growing up there in the 1940s, Foxhome was a small, friendly farming community in the prairie lands of West Central Minnesota – population just a handful over two hundred. Today the population stands at about 115. Sadly, America's smaller farming towns continue to fade away like sepia-toned photos on a dusty attic shelf. That's the price of the natural evolution of modern technology, I guess. Time marches on, and with it, the relics of our history.

At three city blocks wide and twelve blocks long, Foxhome was a typical midwest farming village of that era. It was home to three wealthy churches, Catholic, Lutheran, and Methodist, along with an elementary school for grades one through eight, three bars, and one liquor store. Our little town also had three filling stations that stocked an assortment of bulk oil products for the various farming equipment used by land owners. The nearest town of any real size was about twelve miles to the east: Fergus Falls, population 12,000.

Located three miles into the Great Plains Prairie, Foxhome lies in the ancient land that was once the glacial Lake Agassiz. As the huge ice sheet dissolved into smaller lakes about a thousand years ago, the fine, claylike silt lake bed that was left behind gave the valley its very fertile soil. Just at the tip of the Red River Valley, the earth in Foxhome was an eighteen-inch-thick layer of black, sandy loam – some of the best in the nation for growing crops. In the 1920s, Foxhome was known for its production of prairie hay, what we now know as mature Kentucky Bluegrass. It was considered the hay capital of the world.

There was also a Northern Pacific Railroad depot in Foxhome, with a full-time depot agent and two freight trains that traveled daily in each direction. Our depot also included a passenger train we called the Galloping Goose. It was a one-car oddity with a diesel engine that sputtered and spewed out pungent fumes as it seemed to waddle down the tracks like a Disney cartoon character. It had a railway express compartment, a U.S. Post Office section – complete with postmaster on board – and a passenger compartment with about a dozen seats. It made two trips a day, one east and one west.

◆

Though many kids dream of being a police officer when they grow up, I never gave law enforcement a thought until I was in college. It was the late 1950s and I was attending the all-male St. John's University in Collegeville, Minnesota. My sister, Mary, had encouraged me to attend St. John's. She was four years older and I considered her my protector of sorts. She looked after me and I looked up to her. She graduated from St. Benedict's, the women's college, in the spring of 1955, and I started at St. John's in the fall of that year.

During one winter college break, I hitchhiked the 135 miles home to Foxhome on a cold Saturday morning. I didn't have my own car at the time because we were a low-income family. And in those days students couldn't have vehicles on campus unless they were at least twenty-five years of age *and* a veteran. I could've taken the bus, but that meant cutting into my beer money. So, even though it was rainy and cold, thumbing it was my way home.

Thankfully, I was lucky to get a ride with a Minnesota parole officer for most of the trip. He was a friendly guy who looked to be somewhere in his mid-thirties, and he was headed to Fergus Falls. He liked to talk, which really helped to take the edge off a few hours in a car with a stranger.

We discussed religion – he was Jewish, I'm Catholic. He was very knowledgable for someone so young, and he spoke with a gracious tone that showed a respect for our differences. "Basically," he said to me after several minutes, "when it comes right down to it we're praying to the same God." With that and a warm smile he politely wrapped up our conversation on religion.

I told him all about college life at St. John's, about the interesting sociology and political science classes I was taking. He told me about his job in law enforcement and what it was like working in the Corrections profession. My interest must have been obvious, as he did his best to give me a detailed view of the incarceration side of our vast judicial system. He outlined the several job classifications of correctional work, including the law enforcement element, the prison medical staff, parole agents, and the counseling arm of Corrections. As he spoke, I felt he was unapologetically proud of his career choice. So often you run across folks who'll tell you they *work* here or there, and that's the end of the conversation. But this guy obviously saw it as more than just a job, and that intrigued me. I wanted a career I could be just as passionate about, but I also wanted a good future.

"Oh, it's a secure job, all right," he assured me. "Corrections is a very good lifetime career choice because there will always be law breakers in the world." True enough.

Listening to him talk about his work, I came away with a new goal. It's not that my chatty chauffeur gave me any news flash. I'd already recognized Corrections to be an honorable vocation. It was his pride in the profession that appealed to me.

Corrections has long been a misunderstood element of the public safety equation. This concept of locking up the bad guys has been a controversial topic since the first criminal helped himself to what didn't belong to him. But it's a necessity to an even greater mission – maintaining safe communities for the law-abiding segment of society. For me, the profession reflected a nobility that is sometimes downplayed or ignored outright – mostly by Hollywood productions or an uneducated media. I knew I wanted to be a part of something where I could make a difference. Corrections was that something.

But before I could embark on my career choice, I wanted to serve my country. Though my folks never expressed a thought one way or the other about me serving in the military, I felt a compelling urge to do my duty, as my dad and my brother Lynn had before me.

I had served two years in the Reserve Officers Training Corp (ROTC) at St. John's College, so after graduation I enlisted in the Army and received my basic training at Fort Leonard Wood in the Missouri Ozarks. I received advanced training and remained stationed for two years with the 1st Division at Fort Riley, Kansas. Later, as a correctional officer in California, I would serve seven years in the 91st Reserve Division as a Basic Training instructor. I discharged from the Army as a corporal in January 1958.

Fresh out of the military, I rode with my parents to California to visit my three brothers and their families. First up was my brother Gene and his family in San Diego, then my mother's three brothers in the Los Angeles area, and finally my other two brothers, Clare and Lynn, in Sacramento. It was a whirlwind of a family vacation, but when you're coming all the way from Minnesota you've got to make sure to see everybody on your annual trip out west.

About this time, I was feeling the same angst that a lot of college students experience. It was time to be a grownup and start a career – but where and which one? I didn't see many interesting career options beckoning me to stay in the farming communities of Minnesota. Nothing in the local businesses or factories interested me, and I held no passion for farming. I didn't have the money to buy a farm and I was quite sure I didn't want to be someone's farmhand. Ultimately, I think I just wanted to go someplace else, to experience something outside my comfort zone.

A career in Corrections became my goal, thanks in part to my conversation with the Minnesota parole officer. He promised it would be a good, secure choice with a solid retirement plan. Oddly enough, as early as my twenties I was mentally preparing for my golden years. I was determined to chose a career where I could get a solid retirement plan that was much better than the one my father had.

When we kids were young, my mother and father ran a creamery station selling wholesale dairy products to the farmers in our small Minnesota community. But from late 1942 to mid-December 1944, Dad and my Uncle George found work in the WWII defense industry shipyards in Portland, Oregon. They shared a small apartment in St. Helens, about thirty miles north of Portland, and traveled together to work at the shipyards. During his time in Oregon, Dad wrote nearly 150 letters to Mom back home.

My father was never what you'd call a complainer, at least not that we'd witnessed at home. But away from his wife of thirty years and their five children, his letters at times reflected a tone of protest for the difficult life he was living. He was in a location he wasn't fond of – Dad was not a West Coast guy – in a climate he didn't like. And food, fuel, clothing, and most everyday items were rationed due to wartime mandates. Like many, I suppose he'd grown weary of the sacrifices of war. His letters made that all too clear:

I don't like St. Helens; it's dirty, mills of all kinds, smoke & soot. A car standing out gets dirty overnite. Cloudy in mornings, see sun about the time we get up. Very little heat, 60 degrees I guess in the buildings . . . A young lad about 20 is a welder on our ship. He started in as a student welder and now gets $1.05 hr. He quits next Sunday as he has joined the Merchant Marines and will be on ships like the one we are building. One next to us was launched yesterday, ours will go in a few days. About every 4 days one goes out. 45 days to build one. My work is hard at times; then again it's easy. Have to be in most any position above my head and on my head, etc. After I go to work, can't tell if I've got high blood pressure or not, so much noise. There are times one has to talk right in someone's ear to be heard. Some life, eh?

Back in Foxhome at the age of fifty-five, Dad was too old for the military, but knew he needed money to pay off the Depression debt that so many families were bogged down with at that time. And even though my folks struggled a bit financially, Dad had faithfully paid into his union insurance plan. Like clockwork every payday, sixty-five cents of the one dollar and ten cents per hour that he earned went into his health plan. But when it came time for him to collect, it was gone. The union had spent it all. My folks were forced to spend their life savings tending to Dad's medical issues as he aged. Their hardship made a lasting impression on me. I knew I wanted a better future.

◆

In my teen years I had worked as a plumber's apprentice during the summers in Wahpeton, North Dakota to earn money for college. I liked the feeling of accomplishment in plumbing, of having a project in front of me with a beginning, a middle, and an end. You start out with nothing but a pile of pipe and fittings, and when you're done you've plumbed a schoolhouse or a church rec hall. Unfortunately, that feeling of accomplishment doesn't happen in most areas of prison work.

Because there is no clear-cut finished product in Corrections, I wasn't sure if I'd end up regretting my new career choice. For correctional officers, there is no hands-on work, so there's no satisfaction in seeing something through to completion. As a plumber's apprentice, I'd have the layout of a plumbing project, the water supply and waste collection details, a step-by-step plan right in front of me. In Corrections, inmates do their time, come up for parole and, if they're lucky, leave. You don't see any finished product. You may not see them again, unless they reoffend, so you're not really a part of the rehabilitation process. Criminals must choose to rehabilitate. Officers have nothing to do with an inmate's life choices – especially those of career criminals. Those convicts are simply wired differently than other people. They can lean toward substance abuse, sociopathic ideologies, or get-rich-quick schemes that hold more interest for them than the effort behind an honest day's work. Rehabilitation only comes when *they* decide they are through with a life of crime.

Correctional officers keep the peace within a unique community by making sure the inmates follow departmental policies designed to protect *everyone* behind the wall. There are no moments of glory when a plan comes together, like there is in completing a major kitchen replumbing. Then again, getting home unharmed after a shift in a maximum security prison is not to be taken lightly.

Outside influence aside, I credit my oldest brother, Lynn, for nudging me that last step into Corrections. Twenty-two years my senior, he had enlisted in the Marines by the time I entered the family picture.

Lynn was a fine Marine – ramrod straight and all business. As adults, he ended up much taller than me at just over six feet, and he outweighed me by at least fifty pounds. Because he was quite a bit older, I naturally looked up to him when I was growing up. A deep-rooted sense of responsibility and integrity defined his character. Doing the right thing was his life philosophy.

My mother always said it felt as if she'd raised two families, as Lynn was eleven years old before my second brother, Gene, was born, and Gene was eleven when I came along.

At first glance, Gene was a carefree guy who embraced the fun side of life. But a closer look revealed he was smart as a whip and way ahead of his peers. He was serving in WWII during my formative years, but after the war he and I would go pheasant and duck hunting together.

My brother Clare was seven, and my sister, Mary, was about four when I was born – the baby of the family. Since Clare was the brother closest to me in age, we had a lot of fun together fishing, hunting, and playing pool. And I could always count on him to fix my bike whenever it broke down – the almighty test of brotherly love.

In 1955, Lynn retired from the military after twenty-one years as a proud Marine. In his forties, he enrolled at California State University, Sacramento, where he got a degree in sociology. That's when he went to work as a correctional officer at the iconic Folsom State Prison, about twenty-five miles northeast of Sacramento's state Capitol building.

A chance meeting with a parole officer on my way home from college one winter's day definitely stoked the fire in my belly for a career in Corrections. But the standard set by my brother Lynn, and a few inspirational supervisors I'd later meet along the way, helped me gain an appreciation for the complex job that it is.

So, at age twenty-one I traded in my plumber's helper for a set of cell keys and started my employment with the California Department of Corrections (CDC) in February 1959. Joining Lynn at Folsom Prison, my starting salary was $356 per month.

Putting on the uniform on my first day as a correctional officer, I shrugged my shoulders at my reflection in the mirror. What the hell, I'll give it five years. If I hate it I can always go back to plumbing.

CHAPTER TWO

PROS, CONS, AND POTTY WATCH

The legacy of Folsom State Prison is a history-lovers dream. Built to ease an overcrowded San Quentin, Folsom Prison was one of the nation's first maximum security facilities, and the country's first prison to have electricity. Although the prison received its first forty-four inmates from San Quentin in July 1880 and was housing about nine hundred inmates by 1897, the prison didn't have a solid wall surrounding the facility until four decades after the first convicts arrived.

Construction on the thirty-foot granite wall began in 1909, and was finally completed in 1923. The hand-cut blue granite used for the wall was excavated from the on-site quarry by convicts, killing two birds with one stone. The work gave the convicts something to do all day, and tapping into nature's bounty saved the state the cost of the materials. The granite wall was designed to enclose the facility on three sides. The fourth side is actually a natural barrier, the unyielding American River raging below a rocky granite bank.

Inside that granite fortress, Folsom Prison's inmates live in five cell blocks constructed of reinforced concrete, named One Building, Two Building, and so forth. The oldest dates back to the 1880s; the most recent was built in the 1950s. The combined cell blocks could house up to 3,300 inmates. Three of the five buildings were five tiers high. When I was there in the late '50s and early '60s, convicts in many sections were double celled – two men to each cell — increasing the count upwards of a thousand inmates in a single cell block.

In the early 1980s, California was the first state in the nation to develop a standardized prisoner classification system. The system assigned inmates a Level 1, 2, 3, or 4 classification based on several factors, such as an inmate's escape profile, history of violence, and severity of the current offense. Level 1 is considered a minimum custody classification. Level 4 is for inmates needing maximum custody supervision and housing. Before the new system was developed, inmates were simply classified as minimum, medium, close-custody, or max-custody supervision. Two types of inmates can be found in prison: the majority of felons who fall into general population and the high-risk felons needing maximum security.

General population inmates are typically rule-compliant individuals and are not held under any particular restraint inside the prison. In my early days, they were usually repeat offenders, armed robbers, car thieves, and the like. The more dangerous maximum custody prisoners — murderers, kidnappers, cop-killers, gang members — were always housed one man to a cell in the max-security cell blocks.

The general population convicts were required to work in the prison kitchen or laundry services as part of their sentence. It's a common misconception by the public that inmates would love the chance to get their hands on knives and other weapon-like tools found in the industrial prison kitchens. The truth is many inmates don't want anything to do with kitchen work — or any work, for that matter. Though there have been one or two who relished the opportunity.

In the early 1960s, we housed an inmate at Folsom whose stealth use of a kitchen knife would put a high-class restaurant chef to shame. Doing time on a murder conviction, the inmate had a unique fascination with knives of all kinds — the bigger, the better. He was a small Asian guy, only a hair over five feet, somewhere in his late thirties. He had been there awhile.

One very hot Fourth of July weekend, I was working as the food service sergeant when the prison received a special treat for the inmates: a couple of truckloads of whole watermelons from a generous local farmer. I knew it was going to be a pretty big job cutting up about 1,500 melons, so I figured I'd give the job to someone I knew would appreciate it.

My blade-loving convict was thrilled to get the assignment, and he went to work with the verve of a seasoned angler in a fish filleting competition. In fact, his enthusiasm bordered on eroticism. Soon, the prison's silver-toned industrial kitchen was covered in the pink-hued juice of dismembered melons as far as the eye could see, and the countertop and floor were bespeckled with an army of flying black seeds. He made quick work of those melons, which pleased the rest of the population. And I think he enjoyed showing off his skills.

As I watched him gut the hell out of that produce, I had some brief second thoughts about giving a murderer a set of big knives and letting him loose in the kitchen. But it all worked out in the end. It just goes to show the complexity behind managing the many personalities that reside behind prison walls. Sometimes you just have to trust your instincts.

Though the watermelons were trucked in, we did have access to some of our own fresh produce. The rolling, tree-studded foothills that make up the property of Folsom Prison were perfect for raising livestock and harvesting peach trees and other fruits and vegetables. Over the years, the working ranch at Folsom has been home to dairy cattle, hogs, and chickens – as well as the two hundred or so minimum security inmate workers needed to maintain the ranch.

And because criminals will be criminals, two or three times a year an antsy inmate would just walk off the ranch and disappear into the community. Despite the minimum security classification, this was considered escape from prison, according to California Penal Code, a very serious infraction. The offense carried a sentence of an additional six months to five years if the inmate was caught and convicted. Typically, they'd be back on the property in time for dinner.

◆

Every prison must also have a jail within the prison – the area reserved for inmates who flat-out refuse to comply with the rules. Four Building at Folsom was that place – *the Lockup*. Formally known as Administrative Segregation (Ad Seg), the name Lockup also refers to the Adjustment Center (AC) at other facilities, such as San Quentin, or the Security Housing Unit (SHU) at California's Pelican Bay State Prison near the Oregon border. An Ad Seg, AC, or SHU unit also houses maximum security inmates who pose a very real danger to others, inmates awaiting trial, and inmates being held in protective custody.

Some obstinate inmates simply refuse to *program*, meaning they refuse to peacefully do their time and follow the rules. They choose instead to cause trouble. This lapse in judgment can range anywhere from disobeying a direct order, such as refusing to exit their cells upon request, to assaulting or killing a correctional officer or another inmate. Because the rules are intended to keep everyone safe, there is simply no tolerance for disobedience. Violators are quickly transferred from general population to the Lockup to rethink their behavior. In my day, Folsom's Lockup could house up to 138 of the property's most dangerous inmates.

The dark sub-culture of prisoners who reside in the state's Lockup units includes sexual predators, child molesters, serial killers, active gang members trying to recruit new members, and inmates deemed to be a valid threat to staff. These aren't your average felons. The FBI has their Most Wanted list of dangerous criminals, and most of the convicts in the Lockup go a step or two above those.

Retired Folsom Prison Warden Glenn Mueller has accurately described them as "the most treacherous rattlesnakes in the cage."

Treacherous, yes, but also devious. I found it fascinating to try and intercept their toxic plots that always seemed to be simmering like a witch's brew on the back burner. As it turned out, this was the part of the job I loved the most: the reconnaissance and intrigue. Learning to spot certain body language, changes in routines, suspicious eye contact, or nervous behavior became a critical job skill. Though it was a challenge keeping up with their schemes to assault, kill, or escape, it made for an interesting shift.

◆

In correctional facilities, the search procedure for inmates departing or returning to their cells is a meticulous procedure for good reason. This is especially true in max-security cell blocks. Searching cuts down on inmates smuggling contraband, such as drugs, weapons, or ammo.

Smuggling contraband jeopardizes the safety of the entire institution, but just like other rules, some inmates will bend them until they break. And many are pretty darn clever when it comes to secreting away a tool or small weapon in some of the oddest places. Handcuff keys, small tools, or pieces of wire from the print shop have all been found hiding in the belt lining or hem of an inmate's trousers or underwear. Shanks or other stabbing weapons and drug paraphernalia have been found tucked away in the deconstructed heel of a shoe.

Every piece of clothing, every folder of paperwork, even the inmates' hair and genitals are subject to search, especially following a trip to the Visitor Center. A visit with an outsider is a perfect opportunity for an inmate to come into contact with contraband.

In the Lockup, the search procedure begins when a control corridor officer at the front of the tier "throws the bar," using the remote locking system to unlock a cell. The inmate exits the cell and walks to the front of the tier, stopping at the grill gate – a floor-to-ceiling barred gate separating the tier of cells from the corridor, or foyer of the building. An officer stands on the other side of the gate. If the inmate is on his way to the Visitor Center, he is in a T-shirt and undershorts, carrying his denims, shoes, and socks with him. If he is on his way to meet with his attorney in a visiting room, the inmate may also be carrying legal paperwork. At this point, the inmate passes his clothing and paperwork through the gate to the officer, who searches thoroughly, checking seams and hems before placing the items on a table. The inmate walks through the grill gate, stopping just inside it, where he removes his underwear for an unclothed, complete body search. The officer checks through the inmate's underwear, making certain nothing is hidden in the seams and there are no false pockets.

Today, officers wear protective gloves during searches to lessen the exposure to contagious diseases, such as HIV or hepatitis. But in the 1950s, '60s, and '70s there was no thought to protecting officers from such potential threats.

During the unclothed body search, the inmate must raise his arms and fluff his hands through his hair. He lifts his testicles so the officer can look underneath to ensure there is no contraband tucked away in there before bending over and spreading his buttocks to show there is nothing hiding in his anus. Strange as it may sound, searches have been known to uncover handcuff keys and small amounts of hard drugs tucked between buttocks or hiding in thick pubic hair. If those items were to reach an inmate's cell, there's no telling where they might be squirreled away. The inmates can be quite innovative. In one cell search many years ago we found a convict had turned his toilet tissue holder into a secret compartment for drugs. In the carpentry shop, he made a wooden spool that had a hollow center and reverse threads so that it could be unscrewed both ways. Inside the cylinder, we found some cotton, a needle, and a small bit of heroin.

Finally, the inmate being searched raises each foot, revealing nothing is taped to the bottom of his feet before turning to face the officer who does another visual inspection of the head and shoulders.

Each item of clothing is then handed back to the inmate. Once dressed, any paperwork he brought with him from his cell is searched for contraband, just as his clothing was. When the search is over, a yard officer is dispatched to the AC to escort the maximum security inmate to the Visitor Center.

Sequestered in small rooms, Lockup inmates are supervised in their visits by officers stationed outside the rooms. When the visit is over, which can last as long as a couple of hours, the inmate is given a clothed pat-down search and a quick visual search of any materials leaving with the inmate. This is not to have a peek at the documents. No officer has the time to read through an inmate's legal paperwork. Searching any papers or folders traveling with the inmate to his cell is merely done to intercept any contraband that may have been passed to the inmate from his visitor and slipped within the sometimes bulging files of legal papers the inmate takes back to his cell. Nine out of ten times the search would produce nothing worse than indiscreet photographs of a love interest. It's that tenth time you have to worry about.

When an inmate is escorted back to the Lockup the yard officer generally stays to assist the tier officer in another unclothed body search – repeating the search conducted before he left the Lockup unit. Officers pay particular attention to the waistband and hems on the denims, where it might be easy to stash a small knife blade or tiny packet of drugs. His shoes are also examined closely to make sure the heels and soles have not been tampered with.

This detailed search procedure sounds lengthy but in reality takes only five or six minutes. It occurs every time an AC inmate exits his cell – for a medical or dental appointment, to exercise or shower, or to meet with a visitor.

Part of the reasoning behind the strip search, other than to intercept any contraband, is to maintain a concept of control. Everyone feels defenseless when naked in view of others. There's definitely a sense of vulnerability. A naked inmate more readily recognizes the officer as the one in charge; he or she is the boss. This control component is critical in a thorough search, and is done to ensure the safety of everyone living or working behind the wall.

If there was any chance of a particular inmate becoming aggressive during a search, or if the inmate had a history of that behavior, he would be placed in a small holding cage in the common-use foyer immediately upon returning from a visit. He'd be searched visually, unclothed, with a grill gate between him and the officer.

While inmates who are free from their cells carry a greater probability for attack and assault, celled inmates are not without their potential for danger.

Inmates have been known to roll up a sheet of newspaper as tightly as possible and attach to one end any small piece of metal they could find. And just like that, it's a bona fide stabbing weapon. Some inmates show their gratitude for meals by attacking an officer coming around to pick up food trays. When the cell's food port is opened, and the officer reaches in to retrieve the tray, the inmate will quickly grab the wrist of an officer like a Kodiak bear snatching a salmon out of a rushing river. Violently pulling the officer in toward the bars and twisting the wrist can do some major damage, believe me.

◆

At times an inmate's search procedure requires another level of investigation, namely an unpleasant but necessary task known as contraband surveillance watch. In prison terms, potty watch.

If an inmate is seen quickly swallowing something during a visit with outsiders, or if officers suspect contraband has been ingested by an inmate – which happens more than you'd think – the inmate is immediately transferred to a caged holding cell. In my day, that cell was in the front of the Lockup unit, and inside the cell was a stool and a bucket.

The inmate is held under the constant watchful eye of officers – until the contraband works its way through the inmate's digestive system, prompting defecation into the bucket. At that time, an officer dons a pair of medical gloves, removes the bucket from the cell, and examines the feces closely for contraband. He is looking for a plastic baggie or other protective shield filled with drugs.

As a way of getting drugs to an inmate, visitors sometimes hide drugs inside a condom, which is then passed to the inmate who swallows the item to be retrieved later. With a consistency of skin, the latex condom is strong and difficult to detect in an X-ray, making potty watch the only sure option to finding the suspected stash.

Unfortunately, this type of smuggling is not uncommon, and more often than not the drugs are brought in by an inmate's sympathetic parent. It's not unheard of to arrest an inmate's mother for smuggling drugs into a correctional facility – a very serious crime. Sometimes a mother's sympathy can override her good judgment. But rules are rules and even troubled moms must follow them.

As you can well imagine, potty watch is not a desirable assignment.

◆

Those of us in the profession will confirm, most people have no idea of the levels of complexity rooted within the job of correctional officer. Some inmates have a way of cutting right through the crap, literally, giving you an experience in shocking realism you won't soon forget. Their behavior can be reprehensible, disgusting, and sometimes sad.

"Shitty" Freddy was as crazy as a bed bug, but I always had a feeling he was innocent. I don't think I ever felt that way about any other convict in my long career. Freddy was different. He was sentenced to twenty-five years in prison for the attempted rape of a school teacher. But he had always strongly maintained his innocence. And I believed him. I read through his file and the summary of the crime and its extenuating circumstances, and I had to agree with Freddy. But I was not his judge and jury.

Freddy, who was nearing age fifty when I knew him, was a small, thin fellow who looked like he could benefit from a workout at the gym. His job while incarcerated at Folsom State Prison was to maintain the garbage cans on the yard. Each day he washed them out completely and readied them for the next load of trash. He took this responsibility very seriously. He meticulously painted the fifty-five gallon drums a bright green and marked them with a stencil that read YARD in big bold letters. You might say Freddy was on the psychotic fringe about his task. If someone mistreated his cans they would have hell to pay. He walked around that yard policing his trash cans like he was guarding a treasured fleet of shiny expensive automobiles.

Because Freddy would never admit guilt nor show remorse for the crime that sent him to Folsom, he didn't do well in his parole hearings. As his parole hearing dates approached, he'd begin acting out in a strikingly vile way. He'd smear his feces all over his body, hence the nickname *Shitty* Freddy. He made a complete nuisance of himself, angering anyone within a twenty-foot range.

One day in the mid-1960s, California's Governor Pat Brown was on a routine tour of the prison. The governor didn't know it but as he walked down the tier, Freddy was smack in the middle of a tantrum in his cell. In his typical fit of rage, he gathered up a heaping handful of fresh fecal matter and hurled it through the bars just as the governor appeared in front of Freddy's cell. With an unappetizing *splat!*, it landed on the front of the governor's jacket.

"That smells like shit!" the governor called out in disgust.

"That *is* shit, sir," replied the unfazed officer standing next to him. Shortly after the incident, Governor Brown signed a five-percent pay raise for uniformed staff.

Long after I had served my rookie years, that nasty and potentially lethal display of disobedience began to surface as the assault method-of-choice by many convicts in California's prison system. And it's one that has gained in popularity through the years. Gassing, as it is known throughout the profession, is the revolting act of throwing collected cupfuls of bodily fluids at unsuspecting officers as they walk down a tier. Urine, feces, vomit, blood, and semen fly through the air like smelly, dripping lethal bombs headed toward their targets. It's the reason officers in our modern day facilities now wear clear face guards as some protection from the repulsive weapon. And a weapon is exactly what it is.

Human excrement and other bodily substances can expose an officer to HIV or other communicable diseases like Hepatitis B or C. If absorbed through the skin or other tissue, such as inside a nostril, the eyes or the mouth, it can put the officer's life in danger. But gassing is the type of assault that doesn't just endanger the officer. It also impacts the officer's family. Exposed to potentially life-threatening illnesses means no immediate intimate contact with family members, lest you also infect a spouse or child. Unfortunately, gassing has become so commonplace that every day at least one officer is gassed in a California prison. Every correctional officer on his or her way to work must be thinking, "There's a good chance an inmate will throw urine in my face today." The odds are stacked against them and they know it. It's a dirty job but someone's got to do it.

CHAPTER THREE

A FISH OUT OF WATER

A person convicted of a felony for the first time rarely served his sentence at Folsom Prison in the 1960s. The convicts we saw were mostly repeat offenders, career criminals who knew how to do time. Folsom was quiet and orderly in that era. There weren't many violent outbreaks, very few inmate-on-inmate stabbings, and assaults on staff were fairly uncommon. That was partly due to the business attitude of the officers who worked that institution.

When a new busload of convicted felons rolled in the gate, officers matter-of-factly informed the passengers of the Department's specific set of rules of incarceration. Most important among the rules was the job of the armed officer in the gun tower directly above them. It was simple: Step out of line and that officer will fire his weapon.

Warning shots were fired to get inmates to stop an assault on an officer or inmate, or an all-out fight among groups of inmates. And it was not unusual for an uninvolved convict to be hit with ricocheting cement when the bullets hit their target – the walls or the ground. That became the catalyst for the Department's eventual *No Warning Shots* policy several years after my first shift. And today you'll see that message posted or stenciled on the concrete walls of California's prisons. If the inmates start something they may be sorry. Just three little words leave nothing to chance: *No Warning Shots*. Deadly force may be used by officers to stop inmate fights or attacks as a way to save lives. Warning shots can be fired – and have been fired – by today's officers to stop the perpetrators, but it's up to each officer to quickly assess the situation before deciding to fire a weapon, and defend his or her decision later.

Some of the convicts would school the newer convicts coming into the institution, offering advice to make the transition to incarceration easier. Or maybe they just wanted to have a little fun.

"Don't be doing any "gunseling," the self-appointed advisors would say to discourage the newbies from playing the tough-guy role. "Just stay in line and be quiet. Lay back, man, and don't create any waves – or else you'll go into the hole in wheelbarrow fashion!" The thought of an inmate being grabbed by the scruff of the neck, one arm pulled through his legs, and an officer walking him stooped over like a wheelbarrow across the yard to the Lockup would get the other seasoned convicts laughing and cheering. Welcome to state prison.

◆

In the 1950s, and '60s, convicts ran the gamut from simple law violators, such as people writing bad checks on insufficient funds, to auto thieves, armed robbers, and murderers. These days, bad check writers don't usually go to prison. And that one change has shifted the dynamic of the prison environment. Having those low-level, typically non-violent inmates in the facility had a sort of stabilizing effect on the rest of the population. They were usually more mature than most of the other inmates and were not impulsive. Therefore, they served as role models in a way. They could talk reckless inmates down in the heat of an escalating incident. They were skilled at diffusing a smoldering firestorm among a group of inmates, and they certainly didn't create any chaos. Every correctional institution could use that kind of assistance.

Unfortunately, the violent gang influence so prevalent in today's prisons would simply overwhelm the low-level convicts who wanted to exhibit some basic good citizenship. Decades ago, remnants of the "Zoot Suit" race riots from the 1940s were a part of the inmate population. However, none of the influential, hard-core prison gangs, such as the Aryan Brotherhood or the Mexican Mafia, also known as La Eme, that we're seeing today existed when I started in Corrections. By the late 1960s, violent warring gangs were just beginning to be a problem in California's prisons. Naturally, as that component grew, so too did inmate fights and assaults on staff.

In the last few decades, newer prison design plans attempted to address the weakening safety component of the job. Cell designs moved away from open, barred cell fronts to solid steel cell doors in an effort to decrease violent contact between inmate and officer. The modernized remote-control operation of door locks and gates promised to decrease inmate assaults on staff because it limits the contact between the two. Regrettably, the assaults continued. Day after day, year after year. In the era before the Corrections Department began keeping assault statistics, the incidents between officers and inmates were few and far between. But that has changed. Now, not a day goes by that there isn't some act of rebellion on staff within the state's thirty-plus correctional facilities. Currently, an average of nine correctional officers are assaulted in some way every day in California's prisons.

◆

As the newer designs limited the physical contact between inmates and officers, it all but did away with a critical and reliable element in the business of maintaining peace behind the wall — communication between officers and convicts. Barred, open cell fronts gave the opportunity for both staff and inmates to see we're all real people in here. The new solid steel doors did away with the day-to-day contact with inmates that allowed the officers to build some measure of mutual respect with the inmates. If there was something funny in the news, you could both laugh at it. You could debate politics or the stats of favorite sports teams. The important objective was keeping the lines of communication open.

Forty or fifty years ago an officer just walking down the tier, close to the cell front, presented an oft-used opportunity. An inmate felt safe passing along safety infractions he may have heard about, such as planned assaults or escape attempts, without being overheard by the other inmates. It was a form of communication that kept trouble in check. Interestingly, though most of these guys were obviously undesirable citizens, many of them were good prisoners.

Though some call them snitches, I prefer the term *informant.* Correctional employees must listen to the information convicts provide. However, they're not obligated to take action unless it's valuable information related to prison safety. I've always compared the sharing of information in prison to communication outside the wall. If someone noticed a neighbor's house on fire or car being stolen, they'd call the authorities. The same goes in prison. It's just good citizenship within the prison community to alert staff to potential violence or violation.

In my experience, the news received from informants was usually spot on – and most never asked for special privilege as a result of sharing the info with me. I never went to an informant asking for anything. I didn't have to – they always came to me, some more often than others. We housed an informant at Folsom who answered to the nickname Unit 99. The convicts tagged him with that because he was like a street cop's patrol car, always on the lookout for something to report.

Occasionally, informants share information in the hope of currying favor with a staff member to get an extra serving at breakfast. Many years ago, one of my informants started to report with some regularity the inmate-made knives he was finding hidden in different places around the institution. But his detective skills began to stand out like a forehead pimple on prom night.

One day he said to me, "Nelson, there's a shank on the fifth tier, stashed behind the telephone box." I took a look and sure enough, there it was. I went back to the informant and said, "You keep making these things and hiding them to make yourself look good, don't you?" His eyes got as big as saucers and his mouth dropped open. He knew I was on to him.

Sometimes, an inmate can be so fearful of an impending attack by another inmate that he'll cut himself, self-mutilate, to necessitate a trip to the prison hospital. There, he'd feel safe to alert staff to a wicked plot without nearby enemies witnessing his hushed discussion with an officer.

Others grow weary of frequent prison lockdowns, where all movement is curtailed due to a perceived threat or immediately following a violent incident. Some prisoners figure if they don't give up some dirt on another inmate and help put a stop to the violence, the institution will likely find itself on another lockdown. During lockdowns, inmates are confined to their cells for who knows how long — something neither staff nor inmates want. Running prisons is challenging enough. A total lockdown increases the workload. Inmates locked in their cells means the general housekeeping chores usually delegated to inmates, such as sweeping floors, peeling potatoes, or yard clean-up, must be absorbed by the officers.

For inmates, a lockdown represents a change in routine. Suddenly the daily activities they've come to rely on for some inkling of normalcy are out the window. The inmates get no time on the yard, no time in the mess hall, just more time behind bars. Their cells become the whole world, as staff go cell to cell, tier after tier, passing out meals to upwards of three thousand inmates for each meal. But it's a small price to pay for the safety a lockdown ensures for everyone when there is a very real threat of violence in the air.

With some convicts, their conscience begins to gnaw on them as their lives tick by in years on an invisible clock of incarceration. They may start feeling some remorse for their crimes. They'll share information with staff about potential incidents or safety infractions around the tier, and they may begin to display a more honorable social conduct. Sometimes, an informant's identity is a complete surprise.

In the early 1970s, a Folsom inmate serving time for the murder of four California Highway Patrol officers became a somewhat reluctant though voluntary informant after a visit with his mother. The young convict, Bobby Davis, confided in his mom a lethal plot he overheard on the cell block. An inmate had somehow smuggled a gun into his cell and was planning to kill all the officers in that cell block. Thankfully, she convinced her son to pass the information on to staff, and a potential tragedy was averted. Who would've thought that a man serving consecutive life sentences for killing four peace officers would inform us about another convict's murderous plot? His decision to do so very likely saved the lives of at least five officers on duty that night.

◆

When I first donned a correctional officer's uniform in 1959 there was no such thing as the correctional officer training academy that currently operates in Galt, California. In my day we had *In-Service Training* handbooks for some guidance, but no structured classroom curriculum. Today, the Richard A. McGee Correctional Training Center prepares cadets for work in the state's adult and juvenile correctional facilities, and Paroles Division through a basic training regimen of up to sixteen weeks of classroom and hands-on scenario-based training. The academy training is then followed by a two-year apprenticeship program (one year on probation) that includes 3,600 hours of on-the-job training.

Fifty years ago, our rookie *training* was quite different. We had a five-day orientation period on the day shift, followed by another six months of probation on rotating day, evening, and night shifts. Not much to go on. With little more than our wit, a whistle, and the assistance of friendly veteran officers, we were expected to pick up the job skills by paying attention and watching our backs.

Though he'd been working at Folsom for five years by the time I arrived at the gate, my brother Lynn didn't give me much advice about working there. He probably thought it best if I figured most of it out on my own. He did, however, talk to others *about* me, as I learned on one of my first days.

I was sent to help supervise the noon meal in the dining room. Inside, eight benches and tables faced the same direction, and each bench could seat sixteen. Inmates would file in and pick up their meal cafeteria-style in the chow line. There was always a big pot of boiled red beans at the end of the serving line. Heavy with onions and seasoned to perfection, it was delicious. "Take all you want, but eat all you take, " I'd tell the convicts as they loaded up their plates. "There'll be no wasting food here."

With full trays in hand, the inmates would walk down the aisle in between the rows of benches and take their seats. They were allowed to segregate themselves, so the white inmates would usually walk down the aisle and veer off to the right, while the black inmates went off to the left to join their groups. Other nationalities filled in where they felt comfortable. Two kitchen worker inmates walked down the center aisle with food carts, passing out bread, hot coffee, and other beverages.

As I entered the dining room, I surveyed the chow line to get a bearing on the room and the movement of the inmates. A large convict named Pat looked up, left the line, and walked toward me. When he was just a foot or two from me he stopped and leaned in slightly. If I didn't know better, I'd have sworn he was about to divulge longheld military secrets. Though I was a rookie, a *fish* officer, I knew enough to listen to this stranger with a guarded ear.

"Young Nelson," he said, sizing me up like I was the new kid on the playground on the first day of school, "I hope you do a good job."

I knew immediately it wasn't a pleasantry as much as it was a dare. What he likely meant as intimidation toward a rookie, I took as a challenge. It only heightened my interest in the profession.

Oh, this is going to be fun, I thought.

◆

As a new officer at Folsom, I made a regular practice of reporting a little early to my assigned post each day to talk to the officer about to go off duty. I thought it might be a good way to learn more details about my duties from the experienced officers before they went off shift. My brother had offered this small but important tip, and I put it to good use.

It usually worked out well, and the officer would share his expertise about working a particular post. Mostly they'd talk about the different personalities of the inmates, pointing out the consistent trouble makers. "Don't ever turn your back on that one," an officer would advise, gesturing toward an inmate on the yard or in the dining hall.

Occasionally, I'd come up against a wall — an officer who just wanted to "do my eight and hit the gate," as we say in the business. No helpful hints, no talk about how his shift went, nothing. He'd walk out the minute his watch was over without so much as a glance my way.

When I was working a post on 21 Tower, I'd relieve a real friendly officer who was always happy to answer my questions about the inmates, the prison, or the profession itself. His knowledge, so generously offered, was extremely helpful in my early days.

But the guy I used to relieve on 10 Tower was the opposite. This was an officer who was quite a bit older than me and already well into retirement – at least mentally. No time for the new guy, he damn near met me on the ladder each day as I was coming up and he was going down! I vowed I'd never be that kind of veteran officer.

As I got to know which of these co-workers had no interest in helping out a rookie, I quit rushing in early to engage them in conversation. You didn't have to hit me over the head. I reported to my post at the assigned shift time and not a minute sooner.

I didn't spend much time on the night shift, as most of the staff were there by choice. Staff approaching retirement had a preference for that time slot. For officers no longer interested in the day-to-day drama of working in a prison, the overnight watch is a good way to decompress before retirement, as there is little to no inmate contact during that shift.

Some of the others on that watch were seniority employees who were going to college during the day or had second jobs outside the prison. An officer I worked with at Folsom in the early 1960s lost his job when the Department found out that he was working evenings at a local bar. In those days, Corrections employees could not own a liquor license and could not be employed in a business that served alcohol.

Although we had no formal training when I started in the profession, we weren't completely without teachable moments. In fact, that's how most of us learned the ropes.

In my rookie year as a floor officer I was tasked with assisting another officer in removing a drunk inmate from his cell in the max-security cell block. The inmate, a fellow affectionately known as Indian John, was a huge Native American whose violent tendencies made a loud, ugly appearance when he consumed his homemade brew.

Pruno, as it's referred to in prison, is usually made from fresh fruit that is crushed, added to water and a yeast product, and left to ferment. After meals, inmates were allowed to leave the dining hall with one banana, orange, apple, or some other whole fruit to be consumed later. They could take as much bread as they wanted to the table, but they had to consume it all right there. We were trying to discourage their interest in pruno. It didn't always work. With the fruit in one hand, some would sneak out a chunk of fresh bread still smelling of yeast from the prison bakery as a starter for their home brew. In the days before cells were equipped with running hot water, a tier tender would come by in the morning and give each of his fellow inmates a few ladles of hot water in an empty gallon can. Most inmates used this for washing up or to make coffee in their cells.

But some inmates instead used the cans to "cook up" pruno. The protective coating manufacturers placed on the inside of fruit cans that ensured the freshness of the product also helped to keep the pruno fresh, as nature took its course and the brew secretly developed under the bunks in their cells.

As one could guess, fermenting and consuming homemade alcohol is highly forbidden inside a correctional setting for good reason. Most of these folks certainly don't need any outside stimulant. No matter, the illicit process still goes on today. While some officers simply look the other way, I always considered cooking pruno a serious infraction. Many convicts are in prison because of substance abuse, and can become violent when inebriated as history has shown.

Many years ago, a civilian manufacturing supervisor working in the furniture factory of the prison foolishly allowed inmates to make pruno on Friday afternoons. I suppose he thought they deserved a perk. He'd shut down the factory for about three hours and let the inmates party. During one of those Friday festivities, the intoxicated inmates thanked the supervisor by killing him in a drunken rage.

In the early 1980s, an officer working in the prison laundry was murdered by drunk inmates who had secretly made a batch of pruno in the laundry building. One inmate convinced three others to tie weight-lifting equipment into one leg of a pair of trousers, which they then used to beat the officer to death.

Some people just can't hold their liquor. That's not a concept exclusive to prison communities. I guess some things in life are the same no matter what side of the wall you're on. But the rule is no alcohol of any kind — whether smuggled in as contraband or cooked up in a cell while the rest of the tier slept. That restriction didn't stop Indian John.

"You're all a bunch of cowards and punks!" he yelled down the tier to staff and his fellow sleepless inmates. By this time he was completely drunk and disorderly.

"Shut the fuck up!" some of the inmates yelled back, angered by the rude awakening. This could go on all night, I thought. We knew Indian John had to be isolated and silenced or the inmates in his cell block would rough him up in retaliation the next time they could get close to him.

Though they may be unlawful members of society, the majority of inmates simply want a quiet, peaceful environment so they can do their time in relative comfort. An obstinate inmate making noise in the cell block at night would quickly be admonished by the others. The next day the angry inmates would give him a thumping in the showers. This is their home too, often for the rest of their lives. They just want their neighborhood quiet at night like the rest of us.

My sergeant and I knew we had to lock up Indian John in one of the specifically designed quiet cells at the end of the tier for his own safety. When the other inmates begin yelling at staff to "Kill that bastard!" we know it's time to move somebody to a quiet cell. In its simplest terms, it's a timeout for unruly felons.

To eliminate the possibility of an inmate becoming destructive inside a quiet cell, the cells have been stripped of everything, including a mattress and all bedding, until the end of the day when it comes time for lights out. There is no mirror, no sink, no toilet – only a hole in the floor with a push button for flushing. All plumbing is concealed under the floor. The stripped-down dwelling eliminates the temptation to bang on the furnishings like a petulant child sent to his room. An inmate moved to a quiet cell is given a medical once-over every day, and is checked on by staff every hour to make sure he's compliant.

Up to this point I was an untested officer when it came to physically restraining a problem inmate, and I wasn't looking forward to cutting my teeth on Indian John. He easily doubled my body weight of about 150 lbs. And with the added machismo that a gut full of pruno will give a guy, we might as well have been going up against an angry grizzly bear prematurely awakened from his winter nap.

Indian John was refusing to exit his cell, even after my sergeant spent considerable time trying to talk him out. Like me, Sergeant Clarence Hix was a Minnesota farm boy. He was extremely physically fit, and he was firm but fair with the inmates. They respected him for that, and few tested his fairness level. Woe be to the foolish inmate who crossed Sergeant Hix! That unfortunate convict would find himself in the Lockup where he'd have time to contemplate his poor decision-making skills.

Hix was also a respected supervisor and an excellent trainer. He took a real interest in training the rookie officers, and he knew that plant inside and out. I had a special fondness for him as he taught me a lot about the legacy of old Folsom Prison and the business of Corrections.

Eventually Indian John gave in to the sergeant's coaxing and walked out of the cell as requested. But almost immediately he became combative, flailing his arms and towering over us both in menacing fashion. Sergeant Hix got hold of his arms, but Indian John continued to struggle violently. His upper-body strength was suddenly his super power, and gaining control of him was like trying to lasso an uncaged wild animal. Instinctively, I threw myself on Indian John's back and with a chokehold I rode him to the floor like I was riding a bull in a dusty arena. My theatrical move shocked us all, but I knew something had to be done quickly.

That reflex action possibly saved us from great bodily injury, as Indian John could have easily thrown one or both of us against the wall at any time. Finally, he either ran out of steam or realized he wasn't going to win this fight and he stopped struggling. I used a standard wrestling hold called a Half Nelson as a way to put Indian John on the ground, and no one was more suprised than I was when it worked. Admitting defeat, Indian John complied with our orders and we walked him off to the Lockup unit.

Later, Sergeant Hix thanked me and praised my actions in bringing the incident with Indian John to a peaceful conclusion. From that point on I was considered one of the guys who could be counted on in an emergency. I can't stress enough how important it is behind prison walls to know your fellow officers have your back. It was a significant moment in my early training. I felt proud and grateful for my instincts to jump in with both feet, so to speak, to bring the inmate under control.

Unfortunately, inmates are quick to tag someone with a nickname – both staff and other inmates – and they usually stick like glue. Forever after that incident I was known as Half Nelson, and my brother Lynn soon found himself answering to Full Nelson. I was beginning to understand the oddities of prison life.

CHAPTER FOUR

"IF YOU SEE SOMETHING, DO SOMETHING"

When I was assigned to the evening shift at the end of my probationary period at Folsom Prison, I made it a point to engage in any learning experience that came my way. I had the good sense to know this would help solidify my value in the eyes of my supervisors.

I paid close attention to my surroundings and made it a point to keep my eyes and ears open and my hands busy. If I noticed something that needed to be done, I just went ahead and did it. I didn't bother to check with a supervisor beforehand. Though it was mostly housekeeping duties, such as hiring an inmate crew to clean and restore murals on the prison walls, it contributed to a bigger objective: keeping the peace. The historical art pieces had suffered at the hands of inmate graffiti artists, also known as taggers. Territorial messages of arrogance and gang rhetoric can incite inmate fights in the blink of an eye. The murals had to be restored and the inmate crew needed a job. A win-win situation.

Because of that proactive working philosophy, it wasn't long before I came to the attention of my superiors. Eventually, I earned some choice assignments where I could build on my expertise.

One such assignment was Search and Escort. That gave me the freedom to roam the property for three or four hours searching for contraband or other evidence of malicious plots in the making. I'd meticulously search the lower maintenance yard near the vocational buildings, the license plate factory, and the cannery. I'd bring up buckets of small weapons, pilfered tools, lock-picking devices, *Playboy* magazines, and bottles of booze hidden away for future clandestine meetings. Most of the vocational supervisors — civilian staff — weren't too happy about officers on the prowl for contraband, as some of it was brought in by them for the convicts. But the officers knew those items often led to escape attempts, inmate fights, or assaults on staff. So out they went.

I also had a set of keys that could unlock any door or personal inmate locker in that area, and every night I'd check it all out in my search duties. The old saying about upkeep being cheaper than repair really fits in Corrections. Staying one step ahead of trouble is much easier than restoring order and mopping up after a major incident.

On one occasion we discovered a homemade rope made from braided clothing with grappling hooks attached on one end. Obviously, someone was looking to break out soon. One of the officers tried it out and it was definitely strong enough to hook over the wall and hold his body weight. We couldn't connect it to any one inmate because it was found in the common use area, so we simply stored it in the captain's office. Some convict — or maybe a group of them — went to a lot of trouble to construct that escape apparatus. You'd think they would have been more careful about hiding it!

I can't take credit for inventing the concept of precautionary maintenance in a prison setting. That tip of the hat goes to a warden who was a generous mentor to me in my early days — and a hero whose principles I respected and adopted as my own.

Folsom Prison Warden Robert A. Heinze was the kind of supervisor who knew how to engage his employees and help them realize their potential. As a rule, Heinze privately interviewed all new hires within their first month or two on the job. He'd call them into his office individually at the end of their shifts, where he'd engage each in lengthy conversation so they could get to know one another. When it was my turn, I spent nearly three hours in his office. We discussed his philosophies about running a prison and what I hoped to get out of my career.

"Prison business is always a good choice," Heinze assured me. "When times are good people are greedy and they're stealing, and when times are bad people are hungry and they're stealing. You'll never get rich, but you'll be able to put food on the table." He was right.

Warden Heinze was confident, honest, and straightforward — three characteristics that make a great leader. And he knew how to cut to the chase.

"There's a move afoot to close San Quentin and Folsom," he said to me, sounding a bit like a detective in a television true crime story. Addressing rumors that had been buzzing about California's two oldest prisons, he declared, "Rest assured, you can feel free to choose a career at Folsom or San Quentin, and you'll be able to retire there, because they're not closing either one of them." He was right again. Sixty years later, they're still open for business.

"You'll find there are a lot of people in this business who don't want to make an effort. They don't want to do anything beyond the basic call of duty," Heinze warned me in our meet-and-greet interview. "But I'm telling you right now, if you see something that needs doing, take the responsibility and do it. The prison will run smoother, safer for it," he promised.

Somewhere in the middle of our conversation I got the distinct feeling that prison work was a matter of great pride to him.

Through his words *and* actions, he tried to instill in his employees the importance of the integrity it takes to do the job.

Heinze had a vacation home in the mountains off Highway 50, near Strawberry, California, on the south fork of the American River. Less than two hours from Folsom Prison, he'd go to this retreat most weekends for some rest and relaxation, taking in some recreation in the casinos of South Lake Tahoe.

Legend has it that one weekend, while sitting in a casino, Heinze recognized a young man who had done some time at the Folsom Ranch, and he struck up a conversation. The fellow told Heinze he had been paroled to Sacramento and had permission from his parole officer to come to Tahoe to look for a job. Heinze wished him well on his job search and gave him a twenty dollar bill to help with a new start in life.

When Heinze returned to his office on Monday morning that prisoner's escape bulletin was on his desk. He had escaped a few days earlier, just walked off the ranch and headed for Tahoe. Warden Heinze promptly wrote himself an adverse action disciplinary report for not recognizing and stopping the prisoner in the casino.

Later in my career, a framed photograph of Warden Heinze hung on the wall of my office as a tribute to a respectable leader who gave me a shining example to follow and a working philosophy I'd carry with me into retirement.

◆

I kept Heinze's advice tucked away in my brain's databank where I could call on it when needed. If I suspected a rule violation or illegal activity was taking place, I didn't wave it away. I jumped on it. *If you see something, do something.* If ignored, violations can lead to something far worse than disobedience. It didn't take long before I became quite good at observation, and I learned to rely heavily on my senses.

A correctional officer uses all of his or her senses walking the yard or down a tier in the Lockup. Staff must be on heightened alert at all times because officers absolutely have to be ready for anything at any moment. That's especially true these days, as the sophistication of inmates and their criminal activity has evolved greatly since I began my career.

Just as a keen sense of smell will alert you to someone brewing up pruno, good hearing will tell you if there are impending problems on the tier. Are the toilets flushing more than usual? That was a tactic used often by frustrated inmates, and typically coming after visits with their legal reps. One by one, cell after cell, the convicts would start flushing their toilets over and over again until the system responded by regurgitating like a classroom full of fourth graders with the stomach flu. It was a defiant act of tyranny that clogged the plumbing system and flooded the tier with sewage, making for a long, miserable night for all.

On the other hand, silence can also be diabolical. Did everyone suddenly get very quiet when you walked by on the yard? That could mean a dastardly plan in the works. Even the inmates rely on their senses to stay a jump ahead of everyone else. Decades ago we housed an inmate who occasionally threw a handful of sand on the floor outside his cell so he could hear when officers were coming down the tier. Makes you wonder what he was up to in his cell, doesn't it? Most of the time it was nothing more than a way to convince himself he had a modicum of control – over something, anything, in his life.

Watching the inmates' mannerisms and facial expressions becomes like second nature to correctional officers. You have to observe the inmates every day to be able to notice a small change in their behavior that may alert you to a possible incident about to happen. As he walked off the tier, did that inmate just put his hand suspiciously on his waistband as if to hide some weapon or other contraband? Is he looking around the room nervously? What are his movements revealing?

In time, officers realize the unofficial job description is part prison guard, part sleuth. Skillful officers learn quickly how to balance those roles to maintain order and safety behind the wall. Clearly, the job of correctional officer isn't for everyone. The smart ones pack it up and leave when they realize they just aren't cut out for it – a responsible move.

Back in the early 1990s, an officer who was about four months into the job came to me one day and said she was confused about the job. Though she assured me she wasn't afraid, she admitted she just didn't feel comfortable on the job.

"Then you might not be suited for it," I bluntly told her. I wasn't trying to sway her one way or the other. Some people make great correctional officers, others don't really fit the mold. An officer who is insecure or fearful on the job is more likely to be assaulted. And a hesitant officer could get somebody else injured or killed by failing to react to a violent situation quickly and properly. He or she must have the courage to override fear and run into harm's way when necessary.

"You really should make up your mind *today* if you're going to stay or resign," I advised her, trying to be a little less curt. To her credit, she acknowledged the importance of self-confidence as a correctional officer, admitted the job wasn't for her, and resigned that day. It was the right decision.

The job requires a unique brand of commitment unlike that in any other profession. It is definitely not for the faint of heart. Convicts, especially those housed in the Lockup, can be extremely clever and conniving. They pay attention to details and routine, close to the point of obsession. Because their behavior and life choices have landed them behind bars, they have power over almost nothing in their lives. And because of that, some will go to great lengths to feel as though they've pulled one over on us.

Years ago, I was working a Search and Escort position on night shift at Folsom. The old cells in Five Building each had one granite step in front of the cell door so officers could step up and peer into the cell through a six-inch by two-inch letter slot in the door. I'd step up, shine a flashlight in the cell to make sure the inmate was there, and go on to check the next one. One night, I looked inside a cell for the inmate, and he wasn't there. I held my flashlight up as close to the opening as I could get it. I moved the light all around inside the cell but could not see him. Then I heard laughter. He had crawled up the wall like a huge long-legged spider – his hands on the doorframe on one side, his feet on the opposite doorframe. He just hung there above the door, out of sight like a bat, just waiting for me to come by. I'll bet he was quite amused practicing that maneuver all day long. The convict's name was Pat. But from then on we all called him Pat the Bat.

CHAPTER FIVE

CATCH ME IF YOU CAN

The fundamental purpose of a correctional facility is to keep convicted felons in prison and out of the surrounding communities. To accomplish that task, prisons use daily inmate counts and a corresponding Daily Movement Sheet (DMS) to determine that all inmates are where they should be – securely inside the walls.

The DMS – easily one of the most essential tools in the prison business – is the Bible of the day-to day functions of a prison. All cell moves, arrivals, departures, inmate job assignment changes, etc., are noted on the DMS. If an inmate paroles, is transferred to another prison, or becomes a threat and must be moved out of general population and into the Lockup, it is recorded on the DMS. It's the only way staff can clear the total count on any given day. The DMS is prepared and amended all day long, any time a move is initiated and recorded. Each area of a prison, each post, each cell block, has a copy of the daily DMS. And some posts keep copies of the DMS from the last thirty days or more.

Part of my routine every morning as a yard officer was to study that DMS as if my life depended on it – because it did. Everyone's life depended on it. If a count doesn't come out right, you've got a missing convict, and he's either in trouble or causing it.

Early in my career, Officer Ben Sweet taught me the importance of keeping up with the DMS. Ben was close to seven feet tall and was fondly known as our Folsom Security Squad. When we needed to get a stubborn inmate out of his cell, Ben would lumber in there like a fictional fairy tale giant and get it done. His towering appearance alone in the shadow of a cell door would be all the coaxing some inmates needed to adhere to the rules!

Ben and I would compare notes at the beginning of our shift. We'd talk about who was on the DMS, which inmate was moving where and so forth. He and I would memorize all the names and numbers of the inmates on that document. Like using flash cards as kids when learning math, we'd soon know who was moving where and why, as well as any new arrivals coming into the institution.

With my homework done, I'd walk up to an inmate just getting off the Corrections Department bus and look him straight in the eye. I'd recite his name, inmate number, and what county he was from. And just like that, the inmate is no longer anonymous. He knew that I knew who he was and what he'd been doing with his life. For some inmates, this transfer of power can be hard to accept. No more invisible criminal on the run. No more terrorizing communities, no more leader of the pack. The power had shifted.

◆

There are different ways to count the inmates in a prison, depending on what time of day it is and where the counting is taking place. And there are several counts taken throughout the day and night. Can't be too careful, you know.

Three times during the day, inmates inside their cells stand at the front of the cell with one hand on the bar. Known as a standing head count, two officers walk down the tier and count the heads. And both officers have to agree on the total at the end of the tier. All tiers are tallied by a sergeant and phoned into the control sergeant, who'd have the count sheet prepared, knowing what the total number should be. The numbers the sergeants call in have to reconcile with the numbers on the DMS. If they don't, it's time for a recount.

With the max-custody prisoners, there are about four additional counts during the overnight hours. Officers walking down the tiers in the Lockup have to see living, breathing flesh to mark the inmate present and accounted for. Blankets have to be seen moving, as a breathing (sometimes snoring) body sleeps underneath. Or, the inmate has to make his presence known by moving an arm or leg out of the blanket, lest the officer wake him up to clear the count. An empty cell discovered during a count can mean a potentially long night searching for a high-risk felon in hiding or on the run. Some things in prison can be modernized but at the end of the day you still have to go down the tier and count heads.

◆

By November 1962 I had passed the promotional exam for sergeant and my name was added to the promotions list. On Sunday, November 25, I was working at Folsom as an acting sergeant. The date is forever etched in my mind, not so much for the serious incident that happened on that date, but for the critical lesson I took from it. It became another working principle that I carried with me throughout my career.

It was sunny and warm for late fall in Northern California – not typical for the weekend after Thanksgiving. Most folks were gearing up for the holidays, decorating their homes, and starting their Christmas shopping.

I was assigned to the control sergeant's position that day, which meant I was responsible for the prison count. When I arrived at work about 3 p.m. I was immediately informed that three inmates had taken a visiting men's choir hostage in the prison chapel. The hostages, who were from the Bethel Temple in Sacramento, were being held at knifepoint.

During the choir's performance, three inmates had rushed down the aisle of the chapel in an attempt to escape. Conrad Becker, an inmate enjoying the performance, jumped up from his seat and tried to stop them. Good intention, bad decision. The three inmates were armed with a pair of scissors fashioned into a stabbing weapon and a sharpened piece of metal. Becker was stabbed at least twice in the chest and died shortly afterward in the prison hospital.

As the chaos unfolded, many of the choir members were able to get to safety outside the chapel. But the three inmates ended up taking seven hostages – two ministers and five members of the choir. Brandishing their crude, inmate-manufactured weapons, they forced the hostages down the hall and into a chaplain's office. The inmates reportedly wanted to exchange the hostages for a wide-open prison front gate and a getaway car just outside it. I knew that was never going to happen.

California has a strict no-hostage policy within its correctional facilities. There is no bargaining under a hostage situation in a state prison. Once a hostage is taken, that person is of no value to the hostage takers and will not be considered a bargaining chip in any negotiations. Inmates are well aware of that, but some still try it, hoping for a break in policy.

I reported to the Control Room and relieved the control sergeant going off shift. The room was directly adjacent to the captain's office, which was set up as the nerve center for those involved in rescuing the hostages. It had a small pass-through window to the Captain's Porch outside, a wood-framed room added to the concrete reinforced structure. This area served as an office for the staff manning the loudspeaker, and the officer assigned to the pass window. Inmates would pick up their institution passes at this window. The paper ducat allowed the general population inmates to go to the hospital, to a work assignment, and other areas around the facility. Occasionally, I'd issue a ducat for one of the handful of old timers we had at Folsom. These guys were nearing their eighties. Some had been there for decades. I'd call the snack bar and tell them I'm sending over a convict; give him a burger and a milkshake. It was a rare and welcome treat.

Going about my duties with the paperwork for the afternoon count, I kept the small window open so I could occasionally check to see if there was any activity around the chapel.

At various times, I observed staff members walking up to a window on the south side of the chapel, about forty yards from where I sat. It looked as though they were trying to negotiate with someone through that window. But as the day wore on, the situation didn't seem to be any closer to a resolution than when it began, at least not from my vantage point.

I continued my calls to each housing unit to receive their counts. We were running about thirty minutes late on the counts, due to the incident at the chapel, but most of the prison staff were aware of it. The institution's alert system was a highly confidential telephone number that would ring all the prison's phones at the same time, so the caller could alert everyone to a dire situation, such as a hostage-taking, in one fell swoop. The ring was steady, not intermittant, and would continue until it was picked up.

There were about 2,700 convicts on the yard at the time the chapel incident erupted, so locking them up pronto became priority number one. As we suspected, when I'd finished my calls to the housing units, one count was three inmates short – the maximum security unit. The missing max-custody inmates were the three who were holding hostages inside the chapel. And they were no run-of-the-mill inmates.

Edward Maher, Edward Vaughn, and Farrell 'Red' Fenton were already serving life terms when they made their bold, violent escape attempt in the chapel. Maher and Vaughn were serving five-years-to-life sentences for first-degree armed robbery. Fenton was serving a life term for second-degree murder and robbery.

Just outside my Control Room window, I could see Corrections Director Richard A. McGee and Warden Robert A. Heinze in the Captain's Porch, deep in conversation about the situation in the chapel. Looking outside to the sun-splashed plaza, I noticed three lieutenants walking toward the chapel wearing long, bulky jackets that seemed much too warm for that day.

"Well, what are we going to do, Bob?" I heard Director McGee ask Warden Heinze, who was as calm and cool as a skilled magician with a trick up his sleeve.

"See those three senior lieutenants walking up from the Commissary Gate?" Heinze motioned toward the walkway outside the window. "Each has a .38 revolver tucked into his belt and they're going to go into the chapel and kill a convict each. This will be over before sundown."

"Uh oh, we may be out of a job come Monday morning," McGee warned Heinze, anticipating an all-out ruckus when the higher-ups got wind of the heavily armed response.

"Dick, I've been on this job for twenty-three years now," the warden replied, "and *every* Monday morning when I go to my office I expect to see that notice on my desk."

Just the sight of the three armed lieutenants walking defiantly up to the dutch door of the chapel was enough to bring the incident to a close. The inmates knew they'd run out of luck.

This will be over before sundown. It was a simple statement delivered with the confidence befitting Warden Heinze, a level of confidence that was inspirational. He knew what had to be done, and by God he got it done. No hesitation. No second-guesses. Just plain old follow-through. About four hours into the escape attempt, the three max-security inmates surrendered their weapons and hostages, and gave up their quest for freedom. Inmate Vaughn later told an officer that when they saw the look on the lieutenants' faces they knew it was over. They knew if they didn't surrender they were going to die right there.

"It's good we stopped it early," Director McGee told newspaper reporters. "Sometimes when these uprisings happen the other prisoners get in a manic state and you can have real trouble on your hands."

Boy, that's the truth. When the mob mentality takes over among a group of rioting inmates, their first target is staff. There's a sense of being anonymous among a crowd of marauders. They feel free to brutalize staff without being singled out as the perpetrator. And they can become very destructive of prison property because it represents oppression to them. Again, that sense of being anonymous takes over. They figure they're not going to be held accountable because it can simply be too difficult to determine who did what. They mistakenly think there will be no consequences because they've already disabled staff, and the insurrection eventually becomes a mob scene. Without restraint, some inmates behave just like a wild, looting mob rioting on city streets after a shocking jury decision or unfavorable sports outcome. We've all seen on television how quickly that kind of scene can turn to uncontrollable chaos.

This will be over before sundown. That one fearless declaration from Warden Heinze those many years ago struck a chord with me and reinforced my philosophy in dealing with emergencies within a prison setting. It became a guiding principle that served me well through the years. It also turned out to be one that would be supremely tested many years later at San Quentin.

◆

During the cold, wet months of December and January in that region of Northern California there is often a heavy fog that settles in at night. With its close proximity to both the rambling American River and the large, recreational Folsom Lake, the prison starts to resemble the set of a horror film when that atmospheric pea soup takes hold.

In 1962 when the foggy season crept in, I was put on *fog-line foot patrol.* Tasked with patrolling from one point to another around the security area of the prison, I kept an eye out for AWOL convicts hiding in the cold dark mist that hugged the buildings. My route was a mile or so. Each trip around the old commissary gate, past four armed towers, and back to the new East Gate took about twenty minutes.

There weren't a lot of places for an inmate to hide out on that route. The terrain was a gentle sloping grassy hill that rolled downward to a sidewalk, a street, more lawn, and finally a chain-link fence. The landscape was well maintained, and a convict would have to be pretty clever to find a hiding spot in that area. But it could be done with an assist from the thickening fog.

I remember one December night when the fog was particularly chilly and dense. It was the kind of cold that seeps right through your thick Department-issued bomber jacket and into your bones.

I was nearing the west end of my usual route. I walked toward the vocational print shop and shined my flashlight in the dark recessed doorway. In the haze of the fog, I saw what appeared to be a motionless figure huddled in a crouching position. My first thought was that an inmate had been killed, his body stashed there like an unwanted stuffed toy thrown into the back of a closet. His sudden movement startled me.

"Hey you, get the hell outta there!" I ordered the inmate, stepping back to ready my stance in case he lunged at me. Immediately, he jumped up and spun toward me – clutching what looked like a .45 caliber handgun in his right hand. This *lifeless* inmate nearly scared the life right out of me! If he was armed, I was in big trouble. I had only my heavy-duty flashlight for protection. But instead of attacking me, he took off running toward the fence. I ran toward a tower to alert staff.

"Convict loose in the area! Shoot him! Shoot him!" I yelled up at Officer Howard Merritt in the tower. "I can't see him!" Merritt hollered back at me, confirming the fog was entirely too thick to see anything that was more than a foot in front of him. But he fired one shot into the air just to get everyone's attention.

A second later, the escaping convict bounced off the chain link fence like a tennis ball hitting the net off the serve. Spooked by Merritt's warning shot, the convict frantically tried to disappear into the fog. Whether he was armed or not, I realized at that point he was more afraid of me than I was of him. He sprinted uphill and I gave chase at a full run. As he ran up the hill opposite the entrance to Five Building, Officer Darrell Sands, who had heard Merritt's warning shot, walked out from the gunwalk to a small balcony. He saw the flash of someone on the run.

"Stop or I'll shoot you on the spot!" Sands called out. The convict stopped on a dime.

As I approached the scene I shouted at the inmate, "Get down on the ground and take off your shoes!" He complied immediately. I ordered him to lie face down on the sidewalk and stay there. In those days we didn't carry any restraint equipment such as handcuffs, so I grabbed his boots and threw each one as far as I could in a different direction. If he was going to be stupid enough to run again he was going to have to do it in his stocking feet!

Numerous staff members who lived in prison housing, including Warden Heinze, responded after hearing the 30-ought-6 rifle shot from the tower. It's difficult *not* to hear that sound, even through a thick blanket of tule fog that is native to this area. They all converged on the scene as the convict was escorted back inside the security area to the Lockup.

That shoeless convict was James Monroe Rudolph, also known as the Green Scarf Bandit, a man who terrorized a community in 1951. Rudolph committed a series of kidnappings and armed robberies in the Los Angeles area, though his home was in Placerville, California. Brandishing a weapon, he broke into the homes of store managers in the middle of the night, drove them to their stores, and forced them to empty their safes. To disguise himself, he wore a green scarf tied around the lower half of his face.

He wasn't your typical armed robber. In one incident, while holding a pistol on the couple, he kindly turned his back as the store manager's wife changed from her nightgown into street clothes for the drive into town. When the couple mentioned their worry at leaving their very young children sleeping in their rooms, Rudolph told them it was too cold outside for children, and they might get hurt if the authorities happened on the scene while he was robbing the store safes. He assured the couple if they cooperated in getting him to the store, he'd have them home safely in thirty minutes or less. And he did.

Unfortunately, the Green Scarf Bandit surprised them again in their kitchen six hours later, scolding them for holding back the contents of a third safe. He kidnapped the couple a second time, drove them to the store, emptied the third safe, and fled.

A few days later he was wounded in a hail of gunfire during another kidnapping and robbery incident. From his hospital bed, Rudolph confessed to numerous charges of armed robbery, kidnapping for purpose of robbery, and false imprisonment. His sentence was five-years-to-life in Folsom Prison. Though California law mandated he could receive a death sentence because two of his kidnapping charges involved bodily injury, Rudolph beat the death penalty by pleading guilty to three felony charges.

But he wasn't too keen on being imprisoned. About seven months after arriving at Folsom, Rudolph and his cell mate attempted a breakout. They cut holes in the iron cell doors, likely with a smuggled hacksaw blade Rudolph retrieved from the print shop where he worked during the day. The two had stuffed their overalls with newspapers, using them as decoys in their bunks. They didn't get far before they were discovered by officers, but the failed attempt didn't lessen Rudolph's desire to escape.

On this December foggy night, when the honor block inmates had been unlocked for communal television time, Rudolph had other plans. Using a homemade key to get back into the print shop gave him access to the tools he needed to cut the window bars directly above the recessed doorway. And that's where I found him crouched down in the corner, hoping to be invisible in the dark haze.

What I thought was a .45 caliber pistol in Rudolph's hand turned out to be a roll of black electrical wire that he'd planned to use to scale the south prison wall and disappear into the night before anyone noticed him missing. Foiled again.

I've often thought if I had just been randomly walking the beat, trying to keep warm in the damp night air, thinking of places I'd rather be instead of giving my route the attention it deserved, the Green Scarf Bandit might have escaped that night and gone on to terrorize others in the community.

Later that night, Warden Heinze came down to the watch office where I was writing up my incident report. He praised my keen alertness and quick action. It was a huge accomplishment to be recognized by a warden, and his words meant the world to me. With only three years in, I was still a relatively new employee. His thanks for a job well done in apprehending Rudolph further enhanced my reputation as an officer who could be counted on in an emergency.

At his arraignment for the attempted escape, Rudolph pleaded not guilty. I was subsequently called to testify in Sacramento Superior Court. The thought of testifying in a California courtroom raised considerable anxiety in this young kid from the Minnesota farmlands. It was a new challenge and a good learning experience. Before my testimony, I asked a trusted advisor, Lieutenant Bill Hogan, how to act and what to do in court. "Just tell the truth and you can't go wrong," was all he said. That's good advice in or out of the courtroom.

So I relayed in detail for the court my actions on that foggy night, after which I was instructed to wait for a possible recall to the stand. Soon the prosecutor came out of the courtroom and informed me that the Green Scarf Bandit had changed his plea to guilty, proving that it's hard to argue with the facts. That's a tough lesson for some convicts.

◆

Folsom was also home to James Bernard, a notorious escape artist with several escapes on his record. One such incident had him jumping from a train in Yolo County while being returned to prison following an escape! Like Rudolph, Bernard was not happy being confined.

Doing time for armed robbery, Bernard was a loner who trusted no one. He had no real friends in prison and stayed mostly to himself, deep in thought, pacing the yard. Knowing him, he was probably planning his next escape attempt.

Bernard was housed "behind the wire," convict jargon for inmates living in the maximum security section for the general population prisoners at Folsom. This section was separated from the rest of the building by heavy chainlink fence on both of the tiers, the stairs and the gunwalk. The fencing was topped by concertina wire, or coiled barbed wire, the precursor to the razor-wire fencing seen in modern day prison and military perimeters. Just the sight of it serves a purpose.

Because of his escape record, Bernard was considered a high-risk inmate and was therefore assigned to the yard crew where we could keep an eye on him all day.

The maximum custody inmates deemed most at risk to attempt escape made up the yard crew. The dozen high-profile inmates hosed down the yard, swept under the bleachers, emptied trash cans, and other assorted maintenance tasks. Though using max-custody inmates in the yard crew escalated the escape potential, it made it very easy to keep an eye on them throughout the day. With several counts during the day, their movement was definitely closely monitored.

Every time I passed him on the yard as he tended to his duties, I'd glance at my watch and give Bernard some sort of greeting.

"Hey Bernard, how's it goin'?" Prisoners always look for a consistent routine from officers as a way of having some measure of control in a place where they have very little if any power. Escape artists in particular would watch our every move to find a weak spot in our routines.

So I continued this process for a few months to make sure Bernard was aware of my pattern. Finally his curiosity got the better of him and he stopped me one day.

"Nelson, why do you look at your watch every time you see me on the yard?"

"Well, Bernard," I gestured toward the captain's office, "one of these days, as sure as we're standing here, the captain is going to ask me, 'What time did you last see Bernard?' and I'll be able to tell him exactly."

After I transferred out of Folsom in 1966, I heard Bernard went missing – again. He was found a day or so later hiding under the chapel floor. He was a determined fellow, I'll give him that. And he wasn't the only one.

Decades ago, a San Quentin inmate working in the prison furniture factory took his penchant for escape to another level. He made detailed arrangements to have himself boxed up as a piece of furniture in the warehouse ready for shipping. Safely tucked away in the box, dreaming of certain freedom, the inmate was loaded onto a truck he was sure was bound for greener pastures.

The truck passed through the prison's sally port vehicle inspection gate and headed out on the road. But somewhere in the middle of the night a ruckus was heard coming from inside the truck. Searching the vehicle, authorities discovered the inmate was upside down in the box he had sealed himself into. He was forced to alert someone to his whereabouts or he would surely have died in that position. He was rescued from his cardboard confines and returned to prison, ending his short quest for freedom. Ironically, the furniture truck was headed for Folsom State Prison!

◆

When the Green Scarf Bandit jumped up out of that darkened doorway in the fog it nearly stopped my heart from beating. But that incident was one of only two events in my long career where I distinctly remember being genuinely frightened on the job. The other incident occurred out on the yard at Folsom, when I had about six years under my belt.

Rumors had been circulating that inmate Joe Morgan was going to start an uprising and take hostages. If anyone could do it, he could. Morgan was a Slavic-American with a shaved head and steely dark eyes. Despite his non-Hispanic heritage, Morgan headed up the prison's hostile Mexican Mafia contingent. His leadership position in that notorious group was said to be the inspiration behind the 1992 film *American Me*. Those gang ties also secured Morgan a spot on my max-custody yard crew. We needed to keep him where he could be observed most hours of the day — for the safety of staff and the other inmates.

Morgan was barely a teenager when he first got involved with street gangs in his Hispanic neighborhood in Southern California. In 1946, at the tender age of sixteen, he bludgeoned to death the husband of his thirty-two-year-old girlfriend and buried the body in a shallow grave. He escaped while awaiting trial, using the identity of a fellow inmate headed for a transfer. He was recaptured and sentenced to nine years at San Quentin. A year after his parole, an armed robbery conviction sent him to Folsom Prison.

A big guy at six feet tall, Morgan was muscular and strong. He took full advantage of the prison barbells and other weightlifting equipment to keep himself in tip-top shape. His athleticism helped him win the title of institutional handball champ. Not bad for an amputee. Morgan was missing a leg.

The disability didn't slow him down much. "Peg Leg" Morgan, as he was known around the facility, wore a wooden prosthesis. Actually we kept three wooden legs at the prison for Morgan. He had a tendency to smuggle handcuff keys and hacksaw blades in his artificial limb. It was a clever trick he picked up while serving time in a county jail, where he led an escape of nearly a dozen inmates through a pipe shaft using tools hidden in his wooden leg.

His search and escort procedure at Folsom Prison had to be more involved than most. Whenever he left the Lockup, officers made sure Morgan changed his leg before entering another building and repeated the routine when he headed back to his cell in the AC. This way officers kept a step ahead of any contraband that might've been secreted away inside his prosthesis.

One day, when the yard had been cleared for the noon meal, I was standing alone in the middle of it watching my crew hosing down the large open area. Supervising a yard of felons, some more muscular than others and a handful more devious than the next, can be a test of wills. Looking around, watching them watching me, I'd have to remind myself daily that I was there to control them and their activity as much as I was there to protect their lives in the event another convict wanted one of them dead.

I turned to see Morgan walking toward me. He was quicker than one might think a one-legged convict could be. He didn't hobble like a man crippled by an old war wound. His skills as a handball champ had apparently kept his joints strong and flexible. He moved quietly and without swagger.

As I watched him cross the yard, those rumors of an attack suddenly flashed through my mind. My busy imagination shot a spear of fear right through me. As he moved closer, I noticed he had a strange look on his face. It was determined and unfamiliar.

Oh, shit, here it comes, I thought, as I felt the color drain from my face. This is it. Six years in the Department and this is how it ends. The closer he got to me, the faster my mind raced. What's my first move? What are my options?

Without being obvious, I surveyed the area around me. I was a sitting duck out there all alone on that asphalt pond. Is he armed with some crude stabbing weapon? Is he looking to impress fellow gang members by assaulting me? Does he even care that the armed gunwalk officers will use their weapons in split-second timing if he attacks me? Before I could clear my head, Morgan was standing in front of me, arms at his side.

"Nelson . . . " he began, pausing just long enough to raise suspicion and my blood pressure, " . . . we're gonna need another broom and dustpan out here."

Holy Hell! I couldn't believe he only wanted to ask me a simple question! Morgan knew full well how intimidating his approach would be. I was relieved and irritated at the same time. Did he really just have an innocent question, or did he give his evil plot a second thought on the walk over, changing his mind at the last minute? I guess I'll never know. But his history, his prison profile, and the rumors of an attack had done their job. It was several minutes before my blood ran warm again through my body.

Unnerving as it was, the experience was a stark reminder that no matter how cautiously you go about your day working in a prison, no correctional officer will go through his or her career unscathed – either physically or emotionally, and sometimes both. At one point or another, officers will either be assaulted in some manner or will witness a serious assault and its gruesome aftermath. Those are just the facts of life in Corrections.

◆

I was working the evening watch at Folsom when I saw my first murder victim. It was 1960 and I was barely a year into the job. Working the seating assignment in the dining room for the evening meal, I made sure all was running smoothly as inmates picked up their meal trays and took their seats.

Scanning the room, I saw four inmates hurrying a wounded inmate on a stretcher down the corridor toward the hospital.

The injured inmate was lying on his back, gasping and convulsing as blood gurgled up from inside his body and trickled down the side of his mouth. His eyes were fixed on something no one else could see. Except for the crimson stains on his cheek, his face was colorless. I saw no wounds on his body, but his chest wore fresh blood stains like they were part of the shirt's fabric. He must have been stabbed in the heart, I remember thinking. And with each labored beat of the wounded muscle his life gushed out of his body like water from a severed garden hose.

Oh my God, what am I doing here? Is this what I'm involved in now? I tried unsuccessfully to erase the image from my mind. I thought about my daily tasks, my work assignment, the inmates walking to the tables with their food trays. None of it worked. The grave realism of the moment had a lasting impact on me. To this day, if I close my eyes I can still see that inmate on the stretcher, much too deep into the throes of death to survive.

He was a young white convict, probably in his early thirties. I don't remember his name or number. I do recall he wasn't a gang member, so it likely wasn't a gang killing. However, he was known as a bully around the cell block. Whoever killed him was likely afraid of him. He might have threatened the wrong person and got himself killed in retaliation.

The grisly sights of violent prison murders are shocking, from your first crime scene to your ninety-first. But no other experience is like the first one. That one stays with you.

CHAPTER SIX

YARD DUTY

In the early 1960s Folsom was the maximum security prison for the state, and there were two hundred-plus inmates doing life without the possibility of parole. These were true lifers. Each of the cell blocks had an emergency lieutenant assigned to it. Lieutenant Bud Moriarty was assigned to One Building where I was working as the block sergeant.

Moriarty was a short man at about 5 feet 6 inches, and he was known by the convicts as Uncle Bud, due to his extremely fair attitude. He was no softie, but if an inmate had received some sort of injustice, Moriarty would see to it that it was corrected in short order. If an inmate had a grievance about being treated unfairly by another officer, or lost his job because of a disagreement with a civilian supervisor, he'd go straight to Moriarty. The inmates respected him and they knew he'd always be fair. They'd plead their case to him, and if they were wrong they'd go into the Lockup. But if they were wronged, he'd go to bat one hundred percent for them.

On the other hand, if an inmate violated a rule, disrespected a staff member or, worse, laid a hand on an officer, the wrath of Moriarty would befall that unfortunate convict. That winding road to equitable supervision ran both ways.

One afternoon when the inmates were lining up to go back to their cells for the main count of the day, I was on the back side of

One Building supervising the line. As I rounded the corner of the building, I saw Lieutenant Moriarty in front of the yard office talking to an inmate. I couldn't make out what they were saying, but it had all the signs of a serious discussion.

They appeared to be talking over one another, unaware of or unconcerned with the increasing volume. Before long, Moriarty was pointing his index finger at the inmate as if the point he was trying to make was scribbled on the end of his finger and he was trying to get it closer to the inmate's range of vision. The inmate put his hands on his waist and seemed to rise up on his toes in a dare.

As quick as a lightning strike, Moriarty grabbed the inmate by the shoulders and snatched him right out of his shoes! Putting him in a headlock, he marched the convict across the yard to the watch office. He did this so quickly that I never got close enough to assist him – not that he needed much assistance. I never learned the reason behind that brief struggle. Moriarty never offered an explanation and I didn't ask.

Though he was revered by many for his leadership skills during his time at Folsom, Moriarty was a tough nut to crack. He was very closed off until he knew he could trust you as a dedicated employee. When my shift ended at 7:30 a.m., I'd meet Moriarty walking down the hill along the outside of Five Building as I was headed up the hill.

"Good morning, Lieutenant," I'd greet him as we passed each other. Without looking up, he'd grunt a half-hearted acknowledgment and keep walking. He must have lots on his mind, I told myself.

I eventually figured out how to get on his best side. After months of observation, it became crystal clear that this guy was looking for serious commitment from his officers. And he had no time for anything less. So I was constantly on the prowl on the tiers, trying to be one step ahead of the inmates and any schemes they might cook up. I was on the lookout for potential trouble I could stop in its tracks. *If you see something, do something.* I worked hard at learning the ins and outs of each assignment I was given. I noted the differences in cell blocks and the inmates residing in them, maintaining a close watch on the scammers. I kept my eyes and ears open and my hands busy throughout my shift.

Moriarty noticed my extra effort, and he began to warm up to me. When he became the yard lieutenant, he specifically asked for me when a yard sergeant's position came up.

Lieutenant Moriarty was that rare supervisor who kept to his business and didn't hover around his employees. He let me be my own boss, working the yard to my style.

Though he was always fair, Moriarty was tough as nails. I quickly came to understand the value of his fairness policy and how it made life easier behind the wall for both inmates and staff. I adopted his working philosophy of strong, yet fair-minded discipline. I only held that yard sergeant position for a couple of years, but it turned out to be one of the best assignments of my forty years in Corrections.

◆

Prisons are designed to be classless societies, wherein the populations are equal and all are expected to follow the same set of rules. That design principle is paramount to keeping the peace within these unique communities. No ethnicity is higher than another, no gang or grouping superior to the next. And the system works, at least in theory.

But unofficial subclasses of prisoners naturally develop behind prison walls, though they're not readily recognized by the Department.

In the decades between 1950 and 1980, the few prison gangs in California's system were not segregated from one another. Mainly involved in non-violent illicit activities, such as gambling, they hadn't yet become the enormous threat to staff or the security of the facility that they morphed into years later when they started violently opposing one another and authority.

As the population outside prison walls became more diverse, so, too, did the population inside prison walls. North and south gangs developed in both the Hispanic and black inmate cultures, while most white gang members aligned themselves with the Aryan Brotherhood, and Asian and Latino inmates started hanging out with their own crowds. It didn't take long before the Department realized that even if *it* wasn't recognizing subclasses within the prison population, the subclasses' members were.

Though there are splintered offshoots representing similar ethnicities or regions, there are currently five main prison gangs in California: Nuestra Familia, Mexican Mafia (La Eme), Black Guerrilla Family, Aryan Brotherhood, and the Nazi Low Riders. And they actively regulate their own versions of commerce and law and order within the confines of prison walls. Correctional facilities must skillfully segregate these violent rival gangs for the safety of everyone within the prison.

Somewhere in the 1950s, the Department of Corrections did acknowledge a segment of the inmate population as an upper class of sorts – a less-than-brilliant move I'd classify as the result of a warm and fuzzy moment within the Department's upper echelon. The administrators decreed a segment of the inmate population could be democratically elected by vote of the general population inmates to represent their interests in various housing and work issues of the prison.

This group of new representatives became known as the Inmate Advisory Council (IAC) – or the Men's Advisory Council, the Women's Advisory Council, or the Resident's Advisory Council, depending on the location. According to the January 2015 edition of the Departmental Operations Manual, the IAC serves a dual purpose:

• to provide inmates of the institution with representation and a voice in administrative deliberations and decisions affecting the welfare and best interest of all inmates; and

• to provide the wardens and their administrative staff a vehicle to communicate administrative actions, and the reasons for same, with general inmate population.

At Folsom in the 1960s, this small group of about eight or ten prisoners was selected to represent the prison population in monthly meetings with the warden. This concept works well in a free and open society, but not so much within the specific confines and procedures of a state prison. I waited for the inevitable.

Before long, these inmate representatives saw themselves as the elite group within the prison. They began to think and act as if they had some bona fide authority in the overall administration of the facility, that they had somehow shifted the direction of power behind the wall. That never happened. The Folsom IAC soon became nothing but a gripe session where participants called for the relaxation of the basic rules that contributed to the good and orderly operation of the prison. I think many of us saw that coming.

The inmate representatives would show their IAC badges to officers, as though they were VIP passes to the fifty-yard line bench at the Super Bowl. Looking for some special consideration, they flashed those paper ID cards and waited for the rewards to pour in. Seeing themselves as the select few, they solicited everything from a jump to the front of the chow line or Friday movie line, to avoiding a disciplinary rule violation report. Most of the line staff I worked with saw the IAC as a negative factor and very much a distraction to their daily duties. But our voices went largely unheard and the group continued.

Back then, the Folsom IAC *office* was a small wooden structure adjacent to One Building, near the domino tables under a tower. Supposedly this meeting room gave the inmate population access to their elected representatives out in the open so any approaching enemies could be easily observed. The IAC representatives would take legitimate inmate complaints directly to the warden, on behalf of the large general population. The grievances mainly involved food choices or clothing, or sometimes the inmates' work assignments. The warden would take each complaint under consideration. Once in awhile an inmate would complain to get an officer's job changed. Those complaints were usually based on an inmate's dislike of a smart observant officer. In my experience, no warden bought into those petty complaints. Instead, they'd suggest the inmates learn to live with it.

In the summer of 1966, I began to notice some unusual inmate traffic into the IAC office. After the prisoners had lined up on the yard and gone into the two mess halls for the noon meal, the asphalt yard was typically closed to inmate traffic so it could be cleaned and washed down by the yard crew. I noticed as the prisoners were lining up for the mess halls, a few would casually stroll over to the IAC office and enter the small building at irregular intervals. However, I never observed anyone leaving until after the washdown was completed and the yard was reopened to inmate traffic.

I became suspicious of some illicit activity going on in there, so as the yard sergeant I devised a plan to get to the bottom of it. I noticed a yard worker inmate we called Navajo always seemed to be loitering just outside the IAC office door. Again, I was suspicious. I knew Navajo to be a prison gambler and bookmaker, and I suspected he was there as a point man. The IAC inmates had assigned him the task of alerting them to an approaching officer.

As I watched the yard empty of prisoners except for a few yard workers going about their clean-up duties, there was Navajo lounging on a domino table in front of the IAC office. Out of sight in the elevated yard shack at the end of the exercise yard, I came up with a plan. Before I made a tour of the yard, I would arrange my ring of yard keys to make certain I had the IAC office door key as the first key on the ring, resting my hand on the ring as it sat on a harness snap on my belt.

Nonchalantly, I'd walk across the yard close to One Building looking for contraband around the bench that ran along the building. Approaching the domino area, I made it a point to always speak to Navajo as I walked right on past the IAC office, as if it weren't even on my mind. I offered an informal "Howdy" in passing. I did this for a few weeks to get Navajo comfortable with my routine.

After about three weeks of this mundane pattern, I felt that Navajo was sufficiently at ease with my daily approach. Again, I made my way along the usual route, with my IAC office door key at my fingertips. When I was directly in front of the door, I quickly unhooked my key ring and jammed the key into the lock. I slammed the door wide open and jumped into the office in a split second.

Just as I thought, the inmates weren't holding any meaningful Advisory Council meeting. Instead, there were two gambling games going on involving more than a dozen inmates. The desk was covered with a blanket to muffle the noise of a card game. Poker chips and a dice game sat on another smaller table. When the door flew open, the startled inmates jumped up and made a mad scramble to hide the cards and dice from view. But the jig was up.

Outside, Navajo had been just as surprised by my actions as the inmates gambling inside the office. But he wasn't dumb enough to try and stop me – not when he was sitting right under a gun tower. Standing just inside the doorway where I could be seen by the tower officer, I grabbed some of the evidence. I took inmate ID cards from those involved and ordered the inmates to report to the Captain's Porch. I secured the office and picked up all the keys to the place until I could give it a detailed search.

The watch commander was somewhat apologetic as he explained there simply were not enough cells in Ad Seg to lock up all the gambling participants. I understood. I really didn't expect to have them locked up simply due to the large number of gamblers involved in the operation. The inmates were written up for gambling, and the IAC office had to be taken down to the bare studs to make sure nothing was hiding inside the walls.

Warden Heinze set forth punishments, including suspending the IAC. I completely dismantled the interior of the IAC office – even taking apart the lighting fixtures, desk lamps, and the electrical wall outlets. I took out sections of drywall where there appeared to be holes in the wall, to make certain no contraband was secreted in this crime scene. My investigation turned up negative, as I found no other contraband other than what they were gambling with when I stormed into the office to surprise them.

I photographed the area of my extensive search in case the inmates returned at a later date, caused some property damage, and tried to accuse me of the destruction. And just as if scripted, that's what they did. Some weeks after the incident when the warden had restored the IAC to some degree of operation, the IAC inmates returned to their office and quickly complained to the warden that I had destroyed the place. He assured the inmates he had checked the place himself after my meticulous search, and if they wanted an office it was their responsibility to keep it up.

I've often wondered how many cigarettes Navajo earned from the IAC inmates to be their point man. I've also wondered what kind of penalty he was subjected to from the gamblers for failing in his basic duty that day.

CHAPTER SEVEN

A FELON BY ANY OTHER NAME

In early September 1966, I had been working a limited-term lieutenant position for some five months. When it became obvious that no permanent position was on the horizon at Folsom, I decided to go shopping for a lieutenant position elsewhere.

I interviewed at the California Institution for Men (CIM) in Chino, later that month. Soon after, however, I found they had used an unauthorized list of candidates from another state prison, also in Southern California, rather than call for a new certified list of eligible candidates. I telephoned the chair of the State Personnel Board and explained my findings as well as my promise to file a complaint over the infraction.

Out of the blue about two months later, I was offered a lieutenant position at the California Rehabilitation Center in Norco (CRC), about fifty miles southeast of Los Angeles. The offer came sight unseen and without an interview.

Now I had a dilemma. Do I accept the appointment and go to work in a prison that I really wasn't interested in, or do I decline the offer and probably not get another position for months, if ever? My steadfastly loyal wife was expecting our third child at the time.

"It's your career, you have to make the decision from your heart," Shirley told me, as she always did whenever I came home with news of a potential opening or job offer. "And if it means a move, I'm going with you," she'd add.

Throughout our marriage, Shirley was often my trustworthy sounding board on issues or changes within the profession. When women were just beginning to work the uniformed jobs within Corrections, I had three female officers in my charge who were complicating my duties by consistently complaining about one another. Each had a story of woe about the other and tried hard to hand their problems off to me. Supervising female officers was new to me, so I didn't have a clue how best to handle the situation. I approached my wife for some guidance.

"Did you say there were three women?" she asked. When I nodded in the affirmative, she said, "Don't do anything." Figuring she was toying with me, I gave her my best *'Thanks for nothing'* look.

"If you have three women, they will resolve it themselves," she explained. "Two of them will eventually come to an agreement, and the third one will ask for and get a job change," she added confidently.

And that's exactly what happened about a week later.

With a joking nature but grateful heart, I asked her many times over the years, "How did I get so lucky in love?" Playing along, Shirley would smile and shrug her shoulders as if she didn't have an answer. We both knew I was indeed the lucky one.

Shirley and I discussed the CRC opportunity further. At her urging, I accepted the promotional offer and we started packing boxes.

I reported for duty on a foggy December 1, while my wife — with a newborn in her arms and two kids at her feet — stayed back to oversee the final packing and the move itself. I hope I told her enough over the years how I appreciated her stamina and support through the twists and turns of my career. Like I said, lucky in love.

When my family arrived in Norco, I could tell by their faces they weren't prepared for this type of community. Riverside County sits alongside San Bernardino County in a region east of Los Angeles known as the Inland Empire. The temperate climate and fertile soil of California, along with its gold rush population influx, contributed early on to create the nation's foremost dairy producer.

A busy hub of dairy farms, the state once held almost half as many cows as people. In 1860 there were 264,000 people in California – and 104,000 cows. By the 1980s there were about 400 dairies in San Bernardino County – the largest milk producing county in the nation. That's a lot of dairy cattle in one area.

Unfortunately, a lot of cows produce a lot of cow urine and manure. And when the two waste products meet, their ingredients – specifically nitrogen and urea – result in an unpleasant invisible stench called ammonia.

The environmental impact on the area was obvious as my family stepped from the car. Due to the damp winter weather, the atmosphere hung heavy with the dairy farm residue. The air around us reeked from the waste of a thousand or more cows. Watching the kids grunt while dramatically plugging their noses, as kids will do, I couldn't help but laugh. What the hell had I gotten us into now?

◆

CRC has so far had three roles in its lifetime. Long before it was considered for a state correctional facility, it opened in 1929 as Lake Norconian Club, a lavish, three-story luxury hotel on seven hundred acres. The swanky resort, which included a manmade lake, golf course, pools, and an airstrip, catered to the Hollywood crowd.

The resort was built by Rex. B. Clark, the founder of the town of Norco. In the early 1920s he purchased fifteen square miles in the middle of nowhere to build a community where people could live off the land, taking advantage of its vast agricultural possibilities. But when a hot mineral spring was discovered on the property in 1924, it set the wheels turning in a different direction in Clark's mind. He pictured a grand resort, "the greatest resort in America," and with the help of his wife's money – she was a Scripps newspaper heiress and founding member of the Sierra Club – he did just that.

The ballroom of the Norconian hotel was richly decorated in chandeliers, marble floors, and hand-painted murals, offering movie stars, dignitaries, and world class athletes a royally elite experience. Frequent guests included Greta Garbo and Clark Gable, Will Rogers, Buster Keaton, Esther Williams, Bing Crosby, and Babe Ruth. Pilot Amelia Earhart used the Norconian airfield to practice takeoffs and landings. When the epic film *Gone with the Wind* premiered in nearby Riverside, the film's director, writers, and studio executives stayed at the Norconian.

Unfortunately, when the Depression reared its ugly head not long after the resort's opening, the "millionaires' playground" suffered significantly. The farms and ranches surrounding the resort were hit hard by the economic downswing. As they died out, so too did the resort's luster.

In December 1941, President Franklin Roosevelt turned the struggling resort into a naval hospital, which became known for its historic advances in the treatment of malaria, polio, and tuberculosis. This time Hollywood's elite came not to stay at the Norconian, but to visit the troops recovering at the facility. When WWII ended, the hospital was decommissioned in November 1949, but reopened in 1951 to treat the wounded soldiers of the Korean War. It closed for good in June 1957. Some would say the Norconian did its best work for the country as a naval hospital.

In 1962 the federal government donated the facility to the state to use as a narcotics addict rehabilitation center – the first state-funded addiction treatment program in the nation.

◆

When I reported for duty in 1966, CRC was a co-ed 2,400-bed prison for convicted drug addicts. The institution was designed as a medium-security prison. Double chain link fencing topped with concertina wire served as the boundaries along the public roads on three sides of the facility. There were no gun towers in those days. The perimeter was covered by an armed officer stationed in a vehicle at each corner of the prison boundaries.

At that time, CRC housed 1,800 male prisoners and 600 female prisoners, though we were required to refer to them as *"residents"* rather than inmates. The folks administering the drug program deeply believed in its promise of rehabilitation. I wasn't as sold on the concept. And I never did get used to the idea of calling a convict a *resident* inside a prison. That's like trying to pick up a turd by the clean end, as the saying goes.

Most of the drug convictions involved heroin in small amounts not for sale. Large scale heroin dealers weren't even considered for the CRC program. The addicts were required to serve a seven-year commitment, during which they were expected to get clean and sober. They'd serve a year and a half inside CRC, followed by a parole of five and a half years outside. During this time a parole board would occasionally evaluate the addicts. If they failed in the program they'd go back to court and be sentenced to state prison under a new felony commitment – not a positive move.

The residents were required to attend group counseling for half a day, every day. In addition, they were also required to work at some of the usual prison maintenance assignments, such as janitorial, laundry, kitchen, and hospital. Half of them worked four hours in the morning and half of them worked four hours in the afternoon, either before or after their long counseling sessions. Though it sounded good on paper, I wasn't impressed.

In my experience, most of the inmates simply said what they thought you wanted to hear, whatever would get them out of the room. Overall I never felt any genuine sincerity behind their efforts. And though the Corrections Department promised to erase the felony drug conviction off their records if they successfully completed the program, even that didn't motivate some of the residents.

It didn't take me long to recognize the seven-year program as an utter failure for the addicts, and a waste of state money. Studies have shown the life expectancy of a drug addict to be about fifteen to twenty years after becoming addicted. It's been my observation that hard-core drug addicts don't usually live much past the age of forty-five. The body and soul just can't take that kind of abuse for long, not to mention the potentially dangerous environments that addicts are usually drawn to. About ninety percent of the ones I encountered at CRC eventually returned to a life of addiction and crime. Not exactly a stunning model of success.

Add to that dismal prediction a superintendent (warden) who had a distinct dislike for the uniformed staff, and I knew I wasn't going to be at CRC for long. Superintendent Roland Wood's aversion for the correctional officer uniform went so deep that officers weren't allowed to wear the uniform in the prison. No uniform hat, no departmental patch, just a plain khaki shirt and trousers. Sworn peace officers in khakis. We looked like we were working at the local hardware store instead of a state prison! No departmental uniform in the facility? Whoever heard of such a thing? This went against everything I respected about the profession. The law enforcement uniform designates a person of authority – exactly the image you need to project with law breakers. That is a bona fide necessity in a prison setting – no matter the convictions or crimes. The distinction eliminates any potential gray area as to exactly who is in charge. The late Warden Louis Nelson (no relation) used to say, "Even hotel doormen wear uniforms for reason of authority."

Besides, I was proud of the fact that I had worked hard to earn the rank of lieutenant. Now this superintendent wasn't going to let me wear my stripes?

"Damn, Boss!" I half-jokingly said to him one day. "I'm sure glad you don't have a dislike for shoes. I'd hate to have to come to work barefoot!" He wasn't amused. I didn't think he would be.

◆

My assignments were usually quite routine and uneventful at CRC. Our biggest on-going battle was keeping the male inmates away from the female inmates – and vice versa. That struggle came to a head on New Year's Day 1968 when a major disturbance in the women's unit gave way to a full night of rioting.

Just after 10 p.m. on January 1, I received a phone call at home from the prison operator telling me to report to the institution due to facility unrest. A riot had broken out and buildings were being burned by rioting residents. The men were storming the women's unit, and according to the operator, the institution was in "complete disorder." That's a phrase no correctional officer wants to hear.

My brother Lynn was also working at CRC at the time, and I knew his night shift would have him on duty when I got the call. I had little concern about his safety, as his time in the Marines gave him considerable combat experience in the South Pacific during WWII. I knew he could take care of himself in a place like CRC and make quick work of restoring order to the facility.

As I was putting on my non-uniform khakis, like I was headed to a sports bar with my buddies instead of into a prison to stop a riot, I made a serious spousal error.

"Get my leather jacket, they might have knives!" I blurted out to my wife. When she gasped, I immediately regretted my choice of words. But the truth was the heavy-duty jacket was just what I would need going into a riot where inmates could be using almost anything as weapons. Angry, violent convicts are known to have a particular fondness for stabbing-type weapons they've manufactured from stolen pieces of plastic or metal.

A leftover from my early Folsom Prison uniform, my leather "Ike" bomber jacket was nearly indestructible. It had been through other skirmishes and survived with nary a scar. I knew it would serve as a much better protective accessory than any khaki shirt and slacks outfit I've ever seen.

We were living in Corona, about six miles from the prison, so it didn't take me long to get there. I parked in the employees' lower lot, entered the prison and proceeded down a long empty hallway. At the end, I opened the heavy security door and walked out onto the yard. My intent was to cross the yard, go up the hill to the women's unit and try to restore order. But the chaos wasn't confined to the women's unit. I'd only gone about fifty yards in the darkness when I heard an angry voice from a group of resident inmates that had rallied on the ballfield about eighty yards behind me.

"There's one of those bastards in khaki! Get him!" I didn't wait around to see how fast they could catch me. I made a hasty retreat back to my car. I drove around the prison, parked in the main lot, and headed straight into the armory. I grabbed a safety helmet and a baton for protection. Early Corrections batons were made of solid hickory by the inmates in the carpentry shops, but the one I grabbed from the armory was an eighteen-inch, solid black plastic baton with a leather strap attached to one end. Like the hickory batons, it could do significant damage when called upon. Hooking my thumb and wrist through the strap to avoid it being grabbed by an inmate, I threw on the helmet and ran out to meet up with other responders. We formed a team of about nine officers and headed toward the women's unit to begin driving out the marauding male convicts and get the women back into their quarters.

When we entered the women's unit gate, I saw Lynn in the gate house with a baseball bat in his hand. When he was alerted to the men charging the women's unit, my brother had jumped in a patrol car and he and another officer drove through the crowd of rioters to the women's unit gate. The officer manning the gate had been severely beaten by the rioters. Brandishing the bat for protection, Lynn and a coworker pushed back the angry mob. Fighting off their advances, the two got the injured officer into their patrol car and drove down the hill to a waiting ambulance.

Back in the women's unit, we apprehended about thirty rioting male inmates. The only holding cells we had were six left over from when the facility functioned as a Navy brig. We needed a holding area, a way to sequester the male rioters, while we continued to mop up the disturbance in the women's unit. Lieutenant 'Red' Wolters suggested locking them up between the unit fences.

Associate Warden 'Nick' Knickelbein, a gentlemanly type of guy and a good leader, wanted to release the male residents back to their dorms. Lieutenant Wolters respectfully disagreed, explaining how the men had rioted and committed felonies, including assault. They're inmates clearly in violation of the rules of the facility, going so far as to create mayhem, and should be dealt with properly, Wolters argued. He was right. Call them residents or convicts, a felon by any other name is still a felon.

Thankfully his explanation convinced the associate warden to rethink his release suggestion. The rioters were moved to an area between the chain-link fences. They remained there under armed guard until buses arrived to transport them to CIM in Chino for disciplinary process.

By this time it was approaching midnight. I proceeded around the north side of the women's unit, where I stumbled upon a couple engaged in a sex act under a large pepper tree.

"Okay, knock it off," I sternly ordered the star-crossed lovers. No response.

"Hey, let's go! Get back to your dorms!" I shouted. When they continued to ignore my direct orders, I walked over to them and firmly tapped the female inmate on the butt with my baton. That got their attention. Half-naked and gleaming with sweat, the male inmate jumped up and ran down the hill into the darkness as the female ran into the women's dorm.

After we'd restored order outside the women's unit, Lieutenant Dale Webb and I were on the north side of the unit looking down the hill into the men's unit. That entire part of the prison was still under riotous siege by the residents. The inmate canteen was on fire and had likely been looted first. The records office had been partially looted, but attempts to set it on fire were unsuccessful. The vocational landscape classroom and green houses were looted and burned, as were other areas of the prison. The destruction to state property was discouraging – not just for the institution, but for the inmate programs that depended on the facilities now badly damaged.

Surveying the area, we observed an inmate attempting to set fire to the outside of the laundry building about fifty yards from us. Armed with a 30-ought-6 rifle, Lieutenant Webb took aim in the darkness and fired. He placed a single warning shot expertly close to the inmate's head. His reaction was so funny that in spite of the serious situation, we laughed out loud! When the officer's bullet hit the building as intended, the startled inmate did a spontaneous back flip, landing on his feet like an Olympic gymnast. Shaking it off like a labrador retriever just out of the bath, he quickly ran into Unit One building. Fortunately, the laundry building survived the inmate's arson attempt.

At around 3 a.m., we moved down the hill onto the ballfield where several hundred residents could be seen roaming around. They weren't causing any damage, but refused to return to their dormitories. A crowd of that size can quickly turn to more dastardly deeds if left alone. Within minutes, then-state Corrections Director Ray Procunier arrived on scene to make an assessment of the riot.

Procunier was a profane, self-aggrandizing man who lacked the basic leadership qualities I looked for in correctional administrators. He consistently gave little to no credit to the hardworking line staff for their obvious part in maintaining safety and security in California's prisons. And his ego often entered the room before he did, offering an image more as a showboating politician than the head of one of the nation's largest state correctional agencies. Years later when he left California to take a job as director of the Texas Department of Corrections, Procunier would tell a reporter, "I believe in democracy as long as I can be the dictator."

Amidst the New Year's Day chaos at CRC, Procunier, true to form, foolishly made a grandstand play by walking out into the middle of the rioting prisoners. It was nearly complete darkness on that ballfield. We had no outdoor stadium lighting in those days. Only a sliver of moon and a few stars offered any light.

When I saw him move toward them I immediately followed, offering cover with my dependable eighteen-inch baton. But Procunier suddenly stopped, turned to me and growled, "Get out of here with that weapon!" In the darkness, he may have thought I had a firearm. Ok, buddy, I thought to myself, it's your ass. But I wasn't going to leave him alone out there, so I stepped back a few feet and stayed put.

His haughty efforts were futile, as the prisoners continued to hollar obscenities to anyone within earshot and refused to go back to their dorms. He's damn lucky they didn't do worse to him for his ridiculous display of bravado. Shortly thereafter, Procunier left the facility.

The rioting inmates had stormed and burned the firehouse that was situated halfway between the men's and women's units. The firehouse was manned by trained convict firefighters. Thankfully, when the riot broke out several hours earlier, the firefighters had the presence of mind to load as much firehouse equipment as possible on the firetrucks and leave the area. With an on-duty, civilian firefighter leading the charge, they went through an emergency gate and parked the fire equipment a safe distance away from the rioters.

◆

At the break of day, when we could see the prison compound more clearly, Captain Huel Morphis came up with a plan to restore order. He placed a small squad of armed officers, me included, on each of the three firetrucks and instructed them to drive into the prison proper. As the trucks slowly rumbled in, an officer on a bullhorn ordered the inmates to return to their dorms, get in their beds and stay there under the threat of gunfire. The residents, now cold, tired, and finally realizing their rampage wasn't going anywhere began returning to their dorms.

I went with a squad of armed officers to check on the activity in Unit Two. These inmates were quite compliant by this time, on their bunks and staying out of trouble. It appeared that most of them hadn't participated in the riot at all. In fact, it was later determined that some of the more mature resident dorm leaders in several of the Unit Two dorms had the good sense to dissuade any potential troublemakers from jumping into the fray. They also set up a makeshift security system to protect their dorms from fire and other destruction at the hands of the marauders. The leaders stationed inmates at windows and doors to keep any "foreigners" out of their dorm. They wanted no part of the melee. Their show of maturity and good citizenship was indeed commendable, given the mob mentality that is a typical byproduct of inmate riots.

INTO HARMS WAY | 95

Because of my rank as lieutenant, I was not assigned to a fixed post but was instead expected to go where needed. As more staff arrived that night, they were assigned to control a specific dorm, and were positioned at front and rear entrances to keep the inmates quiet and calm in the dorms. There's nothing more distracting to officers trying to restore peace and order in a prison than a bunch of non-compliant, rowdy inmates stirring the pot from the safety of their cells.

With my independence, I was able to roam around in search of renegade inmates who may have separated from the main group of rioters. It's an assignment that slightly resembles playing hide-and-seek in the dark of night. I went into the records office to search for convicts hiding under furniture and to check on the damage. Luckily, the arson attempt in that building did not take hold. It was a mess, though. Furniture was knocked over and hundreds of files of inmate records littered the floor and desks as if a tornado had just blown through. But the main structure was still intact.

When the uprising broke out, the rioters attempted to burn and destroy the dorms of the other felons. Knowing they would be targeted, the other felons had armed themselves with clubs made from broken chair legs and other inmate-manufactured weapons. They were able to drive back the rioting addicts, set up a security perimeter around their dorms, and survive the riot without incident.

The inmates of Unit Three were not so compliant. They rallied in the long hallway leading to the dorms and again refused our orders to return to their bunks. Captain Morphis knew he couldn't let that defiance go on any longer. He ordered an officer to fire shots down the hall as a warning – not a simple task as the several hundred inmates boldly held their ground. Unfortunately, one of the rounds hit an inmate, killing him. That was enough for the others to know the captain meant business, and they finally yielded to orders.

Because of the death, a coroner's inquest followed. Morphis and the officer who fired the weapon were called to testify regarding the incident.

Morphis was a tall impressive man with a Southern-boy charm and matching drawl. He took his responsibilities very seriously and expected the same from his staff. He was a natural leader and was rightly respected by his subordinates.

At the inquest the officer who fired the fatal shot was instructed to take the stand and be sworn in for testimony. At that point, Captain Morphis stood up and asked to testify ahead of the correctional officer. The captain took the stand and was sworn in.

"If anyone is to be held responsible for the inmate's death, it is me," he said immediately. Pointing to the surprised officer, Morphis added, "I ordered this officer to shoot down the hallway toward the large group of rioters. He was simply following my direct orders as I led the team of officers to restore order in that prison." Inquest officials ultimately ruled the death justifiable under the circumstances of the incident and the fact that the inmates had refused to follow orders to return to their bunks.

The captain's bold statement may have surprised some in the room, but not me. I found it quite admirable, and it enhanced my respect for him. Just as no reputable leader should expect his officers to do what he isn't prepared to do himself, a great leader takes full responsibility for his direct orders to staff. Morphis was just acting like the leader I knew he was. It gave me another learning experience that I gratefully filed away in my growing cache of dependable working principles.

The staff was put on twelve-hour shifts, and I was finally sent home about 9 a.m. on January 2, with instructions to report back for the 6 p.m. to 6 a.m. shift. When I returned that evening the institution count showed one inmate missing. I figured we got lucky, with only one missing inmate after a full night of rioting by hundreds of these *residents*.

A search of the facility began and after about an hour a call came into the watch office reporting the missing male inmate had been found. He'd been hiding in a closet in the women's unit. When he was discovered by officers, he thanked them profusely for "rescuing" him, explaining that three women knew he was in there and had been having their way with him. He told his rescuers he was "plain worn out" and afraid more female inmates would soon find him!

All in all, CRC was an oddly administered correctional facility, and I never felt as though I fit the mold. I couldn't find much to respect about the program so I started thinking about a transfer.

My first official uniform photo with the Department. Here we go!

The iconic East Gate of Folsom State Prison in Represa, California. Boy, if these walls could talk!

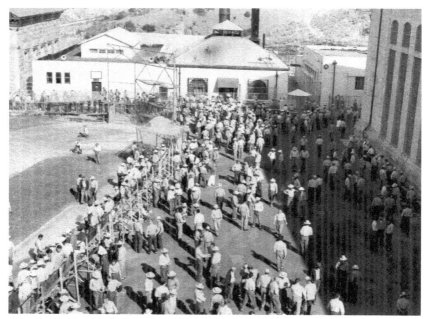

A crowded recreation yard at Folsom Prison, circa 1965.

A rare snowfall in the Northern California foothills town of Represa left a
white blanket on Folsom Prison in January 1962. The National Weather Service
officially measured it as a "trace."

The damage caused by the rioting inmates at the California Rehabilitation Center (CRC) in Norco on New Year's Day 1968 was quite extensive. This classroom and dorm room were all but destroyed. And fire crews had to work hard to extinguish several fires set overnight by the rioters.

My Department photo for San Quentin – ten years in with Corrections, a little older and a bit wiser.

Over the years, I was fortunate to work as a script consultant on several film and television projects that were shot in part at San Quentin and Folsom prisons. I got to work with some pretty famous people, including actor Lee Marvin and director Stanley Kramer. Here I am clowning around between takes with Hollywood icon Mickey Rooney. He was starring in the 1977 film *The Domino Principle*.

The pathway to San Quentin's Inspectoscope Gate, where officers instruct all visitors to walk through the metal-detecting device before they are allowed entrance to the Visitor Center, the tall building just beyond the Gate.

The rules of the Visitor Center are strictly enforced in California prisons, for obvious good reason. Some visitors just can't resist trying to sneak contraband in to an inmate. And that's a danger to everyone.

The visiting area for general population inmates at San Quentin is a large open
area. By contrast, the secure visiting rooms that are used by the maximum
security prisoners deemed too high risk to use the general population area are
secluded and feature steel mesh screens to discourage contraband smuggling.

CHAPTER EIGHT

BASTILLE BY THE BAY

In July 1968, while on vacation, I heard about an open lieutenant position at San Quentin – California's oldest prison. Al Jacobs, my former captain from my days at Folsom Prison – and a man I greatly respected – was now an associate warden at San Quentin.

At Folsom, Jacobs wasn't what you'd call an open book. He was quiet, dispassionate, and all-business. He ran that prison in a no-nonsense way – just like other leaders I had come to admire. I was definitely interested in working with him again, so since I had some time off I completed an application for the lieutenant's position and drove up to San Quentin to let him know I was very interested in the job.

Jacobs was a tall man who did the Corrections uniform justice. Every day he strode through the gate so neatly pressed you'd have thought visiting royal dignitaries were due to arrive at any moment. He even wore his uniform hat during staff meetings and while sitting at his desk in the captain's office. Stoneface Al, as the inmates had dubbed him, was a consummate leader who never had much interest in the pomp and circumstance of a title or position that can sometimes go to a supervisor's head.

While I was a yard sergeant at Folsom Prison in the mid-1960s, then-Corrections Director Walter Dunbar paid a visit to the institution, as agency directors do from time to time. His plan was to meet directly with Jacobs at his desk in the captain's office. However, as soon as the director walked through the door frame the worn eighty-year-old wood floor suddenly gave way beneath him. *Crack!* The sound of the breaking floor boards echoed through the small room like a homerun hitter's bat in the ninth inning. In a small cloud of dust, he found himself standing on the dirt about twenty inches below floor level. Obviously, it took everyone by surprise.

The director recovered quickly and was helped out of the two-foot-wide hole by a couple of officers standing near the doorway. They were careful to avoid any splintered boards that looked as though they could go next.

"No captain deserves to work in these conditions," Dunbar stated, brushing century-old dirt dust off his boots. He immediately ordered a complete remodel of the aging office complex.

Before the project began, a group of us were in a discussion with Captain Jacobs when he was asked how he was going to run the prison during the construction. Without hesitation he replied, "Just give me a clipboard and I'll run this place from second base on the ballfield if I have to." Waving off the fanfare that often comes with positions of leadership – big cars, big corner offices, even bigger egos – he proved he didn't need any more than the basics to keep that place running smoothly. I've used his clever response many times over the years as a reminder of his wit and his example of professionalism.

◆

Shortly after my vacation was over and I was back to work at CRC, I was notified that I had been accepted to fill the vacant lieutenant position at San Quentin. My wife was once again supportive, bless her heart, and once again the bulk of the moving process fell to her. We set our sights on the Bay Area and never looked back. I reported for duty on August 1, 1968.

At San Quentin I felt energized and anxious to dive in and learn the ins and outs of the facility I'd read so much about. As a stalwart history buff, I was excited to start a new chapter in my career at this icon of correctional institutions.

Like other notable prisons across the country – Attica, Sing Sing, Joliet, Folsom, Huntsville, and Alcatraz – San Quentin is a place many have only learned about through Hollywood's dramatic, not entirely authentic portrayals of correctional facilities and the folks who live and work in them. Stories of misunderstood criminals and sadistic guards may have earned millions in entertainment dollars over the last eight decades, but they haven't done much for the profession. That's showbiz, I guess.

San Quentin is home to California's Death Row, where the state's male condemned inmates are housed in three separate areas: North Block, East Block, and for the most dangerous among them, the Adjustment Center. California's female condemned prisoners are housed at the Central California Women's Facility in Chowchilla.

The legacy of San Quentin is not without its controversy, as many new developments were in those early days of horse thieves, cattle rustlers, and desperate miners. Enthusiastic opportunists – rich and poor – were all looking to stake their claims.

The discovery of gold along the banks of Sutter's Creek in Coloma, California, in January 1848 brought a flood of eager beavers to the Golden State in search of those gleaming nuggets. Ships sailed into West Coast waters from all over the world. Sailors from China, South America, Great Britain, and Europe dropped anchor off the coast of San Francisco to join the state's Gold Rush. Abandoning their vessels in the pristine Bay, captains and crews followed the cries of *Gold!* rumbling like thunder down from the foothills.

Unfortunately, where there is money – or in this case, gold – there is also crime. The sparkle of gold dust attracted a great number of unsavory characters. Like yellowjackets to an outdoor picnic, they came. They raided, plundered, and killed in their greedy reach. But while crime flourished, justice floundered.

There were only a few jails around the entire state in the late 1840s – in San Francisco and points southward – and those were hardly up to the challenge. Escapes were a regular occurrence. And the vigilante crime fighters that naturally formed out of desperation only added to the grim picture.

California, not yet a state, was still under Mexican law. Preferring a more influential punishment over time spent in an adobe jail cell, the Mexicans typically chose firing squads for capital punishment. For lesser crimes, the sentences leaned toward flogging, fines, and public work projects.

But as the population grew, the crime rate followed. It soon became clear that California would have to step up its law and order game if it was going to survive the onslaught of traffic the Gold Rush had created.

About that time, a Kentuckian named James Madison Estill who had followed other gold rushers to California, formed a business partnership with Mexican war hero General Mariano Guadalupe Vallejo to explore mutually beneficial opportunities on the thriving West Coast. Estill was a tireless entrepreneur, and Vallejo was a rancher with more than 175,000 acres of land grants in Solano County.

In early 1851, Vallejo presented a plan to the state Legislature to establish and maintain a state prison. He would give the state $137,000 if they moved the state capital from San Jose to his namesake city of Vallejo, about thirty miles northeast of San Francisco.

Vallejo offered the state twenty acres of land on which to build the new prison, and promised his business partner, Estill, would build the prison, staff it, and feed and clothe the convicts. And until the prison was completed, they would provide temporary living quarters for the prisoners on board the abandoned ships in the San Francisco Bay. One such barge was the Waban, a 260-ton wooden ship that dropped anchor in the Golden Gate strait just off the coast at San Francisco in June 1850. Like the others, she and her sailors had come for the riches.

All he and Estill wanted in return for this grand plan, Vallejo assured the legislators, was the opportunity to use convict labor for their other enterprises. As you can imagine, the state jumped at the chance.

In April 1851 they passed an act to provide for securing state prison convicts, and ordered all state sheriffs to deliver their prisoners to Vallejo and Estill. It became effective July 1, 1851, when Vallejo and Estill posted the required $100,000 bond. The only fly in the ointment became the location of the new prison. The Legislature, unhappy with their new accommodations in Vallejo, moved the state capital northeast to Sacramento. With that relocation, the city of Vallejo was also out of the running as the site for the permanent prison. Rapidly losing interest in the project, General Vallejo convinced San Francisco Sheriff Jack Hays to assume control of the state's prisoners.

Hays, a thirty-five-year-old former Texas Ranger, was reportedly one of the most popular men in California at the time. He was a revered figure during the Mexican War, and most people thought he'd make a good lawman.

As part of his sub-lease agreement, he purchased and remodeled the Waban to include cells for prisoners. The ship was docked at Angel Island, just off the Tiburon peninsula. By day the prisoners would work the island's stone quarry for materials to build the permanent prison, and at night they would sleep in their cells on the ship. Reports vary, but somewhere between twenty and forty prisoners were incarcerated on the Waban, under the supervision of five officers. Since the officers didn't wear uniforms, all prisoners had their heads shaved in those early days so they'd be spotted quickly in the event of escape.

And escape was certainly tempting, as the living conditions were far from comfortable. The prisoners were locked below deck in their cells, sometimes four or five men to each eight-foot square cell. In the summertime, the stench of sweating men could be unbearable – for prisoners and officers. In the rainy months, convicts were mandated by Mother Nature to stay below day after day. Escapes and uprisings were likely on everyone's mind.

A few bold escapes and violent incidents, including one involving a group of convicts who made it across the inlet, onto shore, and scattered, began to tarnish the image of Hays as a prison leader. The need for a secure permanent penitentiary was undeniable.

A state prison committee thought a secluded island, such as Angel Island, would serve the best resolution to the escape problem. Unfortunately, all the local islands were heavily constricted by land grants embroiled in title disputes. That's when the committee looked across the sea and noticed the beautiful rolling hills of the peninsula named Punta de Quentin, or Point San Quentin.

This was prime California coastal real estate in what is now an affluent Marin County. San Quentin was named not after a saint, as early California settlers were doing in those days, but after a Coast Miwok Indian warrior named Quintin who fought under Chief Marin.

Upon finding a clear land owner in early July 1852, the state paid $10,000 for twenty acres on the southern shore of the peninsula. Shortly after the purchase, Punta de Quentin became San Quentin. Today, the prison property spans about 275 acres.

Anticipating a financial opportunity, ex-Governor John McDougal had jumped on board the prison project in June 1852 by purchasing a share of the lease and taking over management of the Waban convicts. He had the ship towed to Point San Quentin and dropped anchor.

From there, the story of San Quentin takes off on a winding road through a landscape littered with a myriad of road hazards: unscrupulous contractors, rising construction costs, hard-drinking officers, armed convicts roaming free, a consistently deplorable escape record, and a handful of conniving female prisoners just to keep it interesting.

Finally, the first cell block, dubbed The Stones, was completed and occupied by January 1854 – and quickly categorized as overcrowded. At least it was better than the Waban. However, there was no wall surrounding the prison complex. Escapes were still a big problem, and many resulted in the death or injury of officers and convicts. By the end of 1855, a newly appointed state investigative committee found of the ninety-eight escapes only forty-one had been recaptured. It became obvious that a prison wall was necessary.

Like Folsom Prison, San Quentin's walls are also constructed of granite. However, during construction the granite was found to be a softer quality than that used at Folsom, making it an inferior product. Officials deemed it unacceptable for buildings and perimeters – especially prison walls.

It was decided the walls should instead be poured concrete, about three feet thick. Folklore has it that the construction manager, hoping to squeeze out a bit more money on the project that paid by the foot, poured the West wall a bit longer than the others. This discovery started a state investigation. Prison committee members determined the walls to be of poor quality. They're constructed with salt-water sand, the committee announced, and therefore likely would not stand the test of time. The declaration fell on deaf ears. The claim and the investigation turned out to not be worth even a grain of that salt, as those walls are still standing today – thirty feet tall above ground and twenty feet down into the earth.

Though twenty feet deep may seem like a sufficient barrier, it didn't stop a group of convicts in the mid-1970s from trying to tunnel out of San Quentin. Starting their project in the basement of the North Block, they had an elaborate system of tunnels, lights, and fans. But they had no grading equipment, which meant they were unknowingly tunneling downhill toward the tideline. Fortunately for them, another inmate found out about their plan and ratted them out to staff. It likely saved their lives. If the determined inmates had gone much farther, the tunnel would've filled with water and they would have all drowned.

After the discovery, prison officials had the trench dug open from the outside and hired a concrete company to come in to seal it up good and tight. They poured yards and yards of concrete to fill that gaping hole. Fifty years from now an architect with an expensive set of plans is going to try and build something there and he's going to wonder what the hell happened to the earth!

◆

Our big Victorian at San Quentin was one of eight houses on a hillside street that had been built in the last half of the 1800s. The homes were quite large and many of them had been remodeled several times over the years, adding modern-day updates for style and comfort.

The house offered more than ample square footage for our growing family. It also featured a huge backyard that was terraced into several levels. A wooden gazebo on one level gave us the perfect spot to enjoy our view of the San Francisco Bay. Thorny but fragrant antique rose bushes decorated three of the terraces. Shirley and I took advantage of the unique yard to plant a vegetable garden on one level, and two levels of manicured lawn gave the kids plenty of space to just be kids. And if that wasn't enough, a vacant adjacent lot displayed one old apple tree in the center of the property where the neighborhood kids soon put up a make-shift fort. A handy neighbor later built a kids' playground structure on the lot. It was the busiest place in the neighborhood during weekends and after school.

Across the street, the large Warden's Park offered a spacious lawn next to tennis and basketball courts, surrounded by evergreen shrubbery and trees offering shade in the summer. The park also featured a formal garden of stone arches, statues, and benches – which the kids all took for a cement jungle gym. The area was an excellent place for the smaller children to play hide and seek. The minimum security convicts who maintained the park would be returned to their dorms by the time the packed school buses motored into our community in the afternoon. This removed any parental worry about the safety of unsupervised kids playing in the park.

Our neighborhood was divided into three sections: The Village, The Valley, and The Hill. The Village, just outside the prison's East Gate, was a mix of privately owned homes on the lower hillside, and a row of about five state-owned homes on the upper hillside. The Valley consisted of about fifty-five homes on the western edge of the prison property. These residences were rented mainly to officers, first-line supervisors, and the occasional middle-manager.

We lived on The Hill – also referred to by some as Snob Hill, a nod to San Francisco's elite Nob Hill neighborhood across the Bay. At San Quentin, The Hill was a section of about sixteen homes that included the residences of the warden, the associate wardens, the captains, and a few lieutenants and sergeants thrown in for good measure.

It was an unusual neighborhood in its appearance and population. The streets were very narrow, and the homes had no front yards. The front porches of most homes stepped right out onto the sidewalk like exaggerated drawings in a Dr. Seuss book.

Big roomy homes on small lots seemed to jut up out of the earth, guardians overlooking their bastille by the Bay. It was a different community, for sure. It was a prison community.

The people living there were good people, good neighbors. Even though we worked together we also socialized during holidays and our days off. We'd get together on weekends or in the evenings, sit outside and enjoy a cocktail or two when the Bay Area weather would permit. In small talk, we commented on the sailboats and larger ships coming and going through the Bay on days so pleasant we debated which was bluer, the sky or the ocean.

We watched as military vessels sailed into the San Francisco Bay from Mare Island Naval Shipyard in Vallejo. In deeper conversations, we wondered what their journeys were like and what it meant to live a nautical life. If their sailors could have seen us sitting there on the patio of an old Victorian tucked away on the grounds of an even older state prison, would they wonder what *our* lives were like?

This grand old house begged for lots of holiday decorations, tables full of good food, and rooms full of happy people – and we didn't disappoint. Thanksgiving and Christmas were especially festive occasions at the Nelson homestead. Family poured in from Sacramento and Loomis. Backyard barbecues were doing double duty. Before long, the neighborhood smelled like a restaurant smokehouse. We'd have twenty or more people crowded around our large makeshift buffet table enjoying stuffed turkey, fresh fish, and wild game. It was loud and busy, and I doubt anyone went home hungry.

Our annual open house parties for the neighborhood on Christmas and New Year's Day kept a constant buzz of holiday activity in that Victorian kitchen. Shirley's motto was always "the more the merrier." She made sure anyone who wanted one had a place at our table.

Our house was typically the after-school gathering spot for the San Quentin kids whose parents both worked out of the home. Though we were only a family of six, Shirley would regularly cook enough to feed twelve people. That way, whoever came into the house after school with our kids also got a meal. In the evenings, she and I usually went upstairs after dinner to watch television. We'd smile as we heard the front door open and one of the neighborhood kids exploring in the kitchen to check what was in the fridge or left on the stove for a snack.

On New Year's Eve we'd throw a large party for all our kids and their friends. They were at that awkward age – too old to want to stay home and do nothing but still not old enough to go into town for the party scene. We'd treat them to homemade pizzas, ice cream, party favors, and sparkling cider. I'd make sure to have cozy fires roaring in all three of our fireplaces. Then I'd open the doors and windows so we could listen to the fog horns of the ships on the Bay as the clock struck midnight. Typical New Year's Eve sounds around the area told us we weren't the only ones celebrating in our small community. Even the convicts could be heard whoopin' and hollerin' in the New Year.

CHAPTER NINE

HIDING IN PLAIN SIGHT

In the fall of 1968, I was still very new to the institution, a relative unknown to most of the civilians visiting inmates at the prison. Because of that semi-anonymity, I was the perfect candidate for a special assignment.

One afternoon, Warden Nelson and Associate Warden Jacobs briefed me on a suspected escape plot involving two prisoners housed at San Quentin – John Lynn and Larry Taylor. The two were on trial for killing Lake County Deputy Sheriff William Hoyt during an escape attempt from a Lake County courtroom in October 1967. They were in the Lake County courtroom on charges of escaping a prison farm in September. Lynn and Taylor were led into the courtroom, along with a third inmate, Raymond Pettis. Almost immediately, one of them grabbed another deputy's gun and began firing. Deputy Hoyt, who was unarmed, was hit in the chest. He managed to stumble to a counter, retrieve a weapon and return fire, wounding a prisoner. Hoyt died from his injuries later that day. Eleven days later, Pettis hanged himself in his cell at San Quentin. Lynn and Taylor were left to stand trial for the murder of Deputy Hoyt.

Their reputation for escape attempts followed them like a smoking gun. The plot information, the warden told me, was said to have come from a reliable source. Outsiders – possibly previous visitors – were planning to help Lynn and Taylor escape when they made their appearance in the courtroom in San Francisco.

San Quentin needed a plain-clothes security presence in the back of the courtroom in case something went down. If there were disreputable outsiders sitting in the courtroom, they'd likely scan the room to see who else was there, looking specifically for recognizable faces of law enforcement personnel who might squelch their plans. The warden needed someone who wouldn't be known as an officer from the prison, but someone familiar with a criminal's line of thinking. I was that person.

Each morning I'd draw a 38-caliber pistol with a shoulder holster from the armory. I'd put the weapon and holster in place over my shirt, cover it with my sport coat, and drive into San Francisco's Hall of Justice on Bryant Street. I made sure to be on time – no easy task in the morning traffic. But I knew it was critical to the assignment and extremely important to my warden.

Louis 'Red' Nelson was a former Marine, Alcatraz correctional officer, and a straight shooter who always cut to the chase. I remember one day he asked me and a captain to meet him by his vehicle at 1 p.m. to travel into the city for an appointment. I arrived at 12:55 p.m., and at 1 p.m. the warden came outside to meet us. But he and I waited another ten or fifteen minutes before the captain finally showed up, awkwardly offering a lame excuse for his tardiness. Warden Nelson walked over to him and sized him up and down as if he were his tailor. "Captain," he stated, "when you work in my prison you'll either be an on-time captain or a late lieutenant. Your choice."

◆

As instructed, I arrived at the Hall of Justice each day in plain clothes. Checking in at the main jail, I'd take the elevator down to the public foyer outside the courtrooms. Entering the courtroom as a public spectator, I slyly scanned the room. I took a seat in the back row closest to the door. I had previously met privately with the presiding judge. He knew I would be an armed undercover officer in his courtroom. If an escape attempt was made, it was my job to stop it.

In those days, courtroom metal detectors and the searching of court spectators and their belongings was unheard of. It was assumed that the courts were immune from any violence.

Four days a week, for about three weeks or so, I'd attend the trial, watching from the back of the courtroom. Pretending to be a civilian, I sat waiting for some odd movement or character that might tip off an escape plan. Each time the courtroom doors opened, I devoured the incoming visitor with my eyes. I made mental notes of clothing, accessories, eye contact, and mannerisms. I watched to see where they chose to sit, wondering why they picked that seat, that row, behind that person. Every day I silently analyzed the faces around me in that courtroom, trying hard to get inside the heads of complete strangers. In my mind, I filtered out the unlikely candidates, checking each one off an invisible roster of possible criminally motivated spectators. I kept my eyes on individuals who pulled my focus for some reason or another: the man dressed in dungarees and neatly pressed suit jacket, the young woman with the overly large handbag. Odd-ball fidgety types or those who simply looked out of their element naturally stole my attention. But each day the trial went on as expected without interruption.

Eventually, a well-dressed middle-aged couple who had been the only consistent daily spectators other than myself became inquisitive. During a break in testimony, the woman approached me and asked if I was a policeman, as if that could be the only reason I was there every day.

"No," I answered a little too quickly. "Actually, I'm writing a book and I'm here doing some research." Feeling exposed, I tried to divert their attention from me by asking about their interest in the case, which was starting to rev my curiosity.

"Are you relatives of the defendants?" Looking from his eyes to hers and back again, I searched for a glimmer of something suspicious. Before they could answer, I offered, "If so, it might be an interesting side note to my story." I was lying through my teeth to validate my disguise. I had no idea what the hell I would do if they agreed and asked to be part of the project.

"Oh, we're just friends of the defendants," the woman explained, noting a particular interest in John Lynn, "such an innocent, good-looking young man." As she spoke I got the uneasy feeling that she was deeply infatuated with him. Her interest was leaning away from friendly and right on into prurient. It was an uncomfortable moment.

There's a certain instinct in humans to help someone in need, and predatory-minded criminals are very skilled at identifying and exploiting that instinct in unsuspecting victims. Doing so, they can effectively transfer their problem or situation to the person willing to accept it. Within a prison environment the key to not falling prey to that type of predator is to leave your sympathy at the door. An officer can be empathetic to an inmate's situation, I always told my new officers. Empathy is helpful to understanding the inmate mindset. But being sympathetic is ill-advised. Every correctional employee must learn that. A certain amount of empathy is fine. Sympathy may get you into trouble.

Thankfully, the couple seemed to buy my story about writing a book and didn't ask any more questions. I continued to speculate if they might be part of the rumored escape plan. As each uneventful day passed, I began to wonder if they didn't really believe my story after all. Maybe they cancelled any escape plans based on their suspicions of me. Or were they trying to wait me out, hoping I'd call the coast clear, end my assignment, and not show up one day?

My concerns were unfounded, however, as the trial concluded without incident. John Lynn and Larry Taylor were convicted of second degree murder in the death of Deputy Hoyt. They were sentenced to five-years-to-life in San Quentin's Adjustment Center, which came under my supervision in May 1969.

By the time I was assigned to the AC, the couple in the courtroom who had been infatuated with inmate Lynn had become approved correspondents and visitors for him. My courtroom cover as a writer doing research was blown when they started showing up for visits and noticed me in uniform. Over time, when their advancing age and failing health made it impossible for them to travel to the prison to see Lynn, their visits turned into a few phone calls a month to check on their "Johnny." The couple's almost-daily letters to Lynn were filled with signs of a deep fantasy, confirming my earlier suspicions that their relationship was much more than casual friendship. Who knows where and when this lonely middle-aged couple first encountered Lynn and Taylor, but it was certain the woman had an unhealthy infatuation with a violent killer.

CHAPTER TEN

BELLY OF THE BEAST

San Quentin's Adjustment Center consists of 102 cells. There are three floors housing thirty-four cells each, seventeen cells on each side. The cells are back-to-back construction with a utility corridor running between the two sides of the tier, aptly named north side and south side. On the first floor, the cells are numbered 1-AC-1 through 1-AC-17 on the north, and 1-AC-51 through 1-AC-67 make up the south. The numbers in between belong to cells on the second and third floors of the Lockup.

The last six cells on the first floor are quiet cells. In my day, only those cells featured a solid concrete front and a steel door with a security glass window inset at eye level. An attached steel window flap could instantly give a solid steel cell front. Nowadays, the entire AC consists of solid concrete cell fronts and steel doors. Long gone are the rows of bars where an inmate hung his arms out in conversation with the inmate in the next cell, like neighbors over a backyard fence. Inevitably, as the prison population evolved into a more savvy and violent version of itself, the incarceration environment had to respond through its design. The unique population simply poses too much of a risk.

Meal service for the inmates residing in the AC was a lengthy exercise in safety precaution. The food cart going back and forth from the kitchen to the Lockup was specifically assigned to the Lockup. It remained in the AC to ensure no contraband could be secretly sealed inside the wheels, rubber bumpers, or other moveable parts. In the kitchen, food trays being prepared for the Lockup were meticulously supervised and the food cart was searched upon its arrival in the Lockup. Like many routines behind prison walls, it is time consuming and can be expensive in man hours. But that's a small price to pay when you consider the potential for danger.

Every item coming into the Lockup had to be scanned with the metal detector or physically checked in by officers to ensure no contraband was getting through to the most dangerous convicts in the system. From food and beverages to toiletries and other personal items, anything and everything the inmates purchased through the canteen had to be thoroughly inspected.

If an item coming from the prison canteen was made of metal, Styrofoam, or other material that could be melted down into a hard plastic stabbing weapon, it was not allowed into the Lockup. Instant coffee was taken out of its plastic packaging and put into small plastic bags instead.

In the 1960s toothpaste tubes were still made of aluminum. All-plastic containers for toothpaste weren't manufactured until the 1990s. The aluminum tubes could not successfully go through the metal detector, so they had to be hand-checked by officers. The tubes became an easy vessel for crafty smugglers. Inmates started slipping small stolen hacksaw blades inside the toothpaste tubes, figuring they wouldn't be discovered. An officer would simply give the tube of toothpaste a once-over, and pass it on to the inmate. A hacksaw blade could work quite efficiently as a deadly weapon when it wasn't being used to cut through cell bars in the dead of night.

It didn't take long to understand why the rules were more stringent in the Lockup than within the prison's general population. Given the propensity for disobedience and violence typically exhibited by the maximum security inmates, there were no gray areas when it came to discipline, which made it easier to enforce the rules. The discretionary authority of officers working the AC was very narrow, compared to the other housing units. If an officer working in the general population cell blocks saw a minor infraction, he or she might talk to the inmate before taking any disciplinary action. Minor violations such as grabbing an extra milk or bit of food in the mess hall, not keeping themselves clean, or refusing to stand for the count could get an inmate a stern talking to in place of a disciplinary report. Not so in the Lockup. There, the rules were cut and dried, and they were quickly and strictly enforced.

◆

When 1969 drew to a close, all evidence pointed to a significant year in ways both good and bad. We were paying about thirty-five cents for a gallon of gasoline, the Boeing 747 took its maiden flight, and the battery-powered smoke detector was invented. But Charles Manson and his cult went on a killing spree, and the Cold War continued. Nationwide, hundreds of thousands of people marched *for* civil rights and *against* the Vietnam War. Out in the universe, Astronaut Neil Armstrong walked on the moon, and a billion of us around the world watched or listened in amazement on our television sets or radios.

In August 1969, about 400,000 music lovers converged on a dairy farm in upstate New York for a rock and roll festival called Woodstock. More than thirty artists performed over the course of the three-day event that promoted "three days of peace and music." Jimi Hendrix, Arlo Guthrie, and Joan Baez, among others, performed their hits around the clock. *Rolling Stone* magazine listed the event one of "50 Moments That Changed the History of Rock and Roll."

Not to be outdone, the West Coast responded in December with a free festival and rock concert at the Altamont Speedway in Northern California. The concert was designed to wrap up The

Rolling Stones' very successful 1969 American tour. In addition to The Stones, the event featured a lineup of popular bands of that era: Jefferson Airplane, Santana, and the Grateful Dead. Some people began calling it Woodstock West. However, unlike New York's peaceful Woodstock, the concert at Altamont was marked by considerable violence and destruction. Woodstock West looked more like uncontrolled chaos.

The concert was reported to be ill-designed, and its organizers ill-prepared to handle the magnitude of the security issue behind an event like that. The Hells Angels had been hired by The Rolling Stones (reportedly for $500 worth of beer) to provide event security, mainly crowd control and keeping spectators off the stage. That effort was likely doomed from the start when it was announced the concert would be a free event. Nearly 300,000 people flocked to the Speedway.

At the end of the long day, the The Rolling Stones finally played their set to a crowd now likely swaying less to the music than to the alcohol, LSD, and other recreational drugs said to be on scene. The crowd had gotten more intoxicated and aggressive as the day wore on. Numerous fights broke out involving concert goers and the Hells Angels security detail. The stage, which was supposed to be on a riser, ended up at the bottom of a slope – not an ideal security position. Thousands of drunk or high music lovers on a dark sloping knoll was not a good mix.

At one point, an eighteen-year-old highly intoxicated, black spectator named Meredith Hunter tried to storm the stage. When he was pushed back by security, he pulled a gun from his jacket. Al Passaro, a twenty-one-year-old Hells Angel working security detail, confronted the spectator and a fight ensued.

The clean-shaven, dark-skinned Passaro was not the hulking figure that people might associate with that of a bodyguard – especially a Hells Angel. He was of medium build, not muscular by any means, and easily shy of six feet tall. But he was armed.

In the struggle to keep him off the stage, Passaro fatally stabbed Hunter. According to news reports, an autopsy showed Hunter had a considerable amount of amphetamines in his body at the time of death. Eyewitnesses said he was "falling down drunk."

Passaro was a parolee from Correctional Training Facility in Soledad, also known as Soledad Prison. He was arrested, tried, and acquitted of the killing after it was determined he was acting in self-defense. The crime was inadvertently captured on film in the Rolling Stones documentary *Gimme Shelter* that was being produced about the tour. Footage showed Hunter did indeed have a gun.

When all was said and done, there were three other deaths that night, all accidental, causing some reports to label the concert the "Altamont festival disaster." *Rolling Stone* magazine called it "rock and roll's worst day."

Because his actions at Altamont violated his parole, Passaro was returned to prison, this time at San Quentin. A black man killed by a white man – during a time when racial tension was on the increase inside and outside the prison – didn't help Passaro's case. He was housed in the Lockup under my charge for his safety and the safety of other inmates.

Several weeks after Passaro arrived, I was sitting in the yard lieutenant's office when I was approached by a delegation of Hells Angels inmates who were in San Quentin's general population. They were almost all big burly guys who looked like they needed a shower and a haircut. Though their hair was worn long, beards weren't allowed at the time because of departmental grooming standards. The Hells Angels all carried large leather wallets on chains hooked to their belts. Their inmate identification cards were inside the wallets.

The Angels knew how to do time. They made it as easy as they could on themselves by living by the rules. Disciplinary-free, they lived in the Honor Block, which allowed them to be out of their cells for sixteen hours a day. It also meant they had movie privileges and certain perks in the Visitor Center.

The Angels were all programming without any problems, and I had always had a good relationship with them. I'm a staunch believer in the principle of firm, fair, and consistent supervision, and the inmates under my charge knew this.

"You've got to trust my word, and I've got to trust your word," I'd always told them. "That's all we've got in here." In all my communications with the Hells Angels I made certain that my word was always good – and they had returned the courtesy.

On this day, they asked me to release their friend Passaro from the AC and back into general population. They assured me no problems would come from him being back in the general population with them. Passaro's behavior reflected he was not a racist, and there was no record of any problems with him while incarcerated. He had programmed well at Soledad. And the killing at the Altamont concert was not a racial incident, nor was it blown out of proportion as such by the press during the trial.

So I took their request to Associate Warden Jacobs. Because of the persistent racial unrest within the institution, we were always in need of additional AC maximum security cells to house combative inmates. We were continually looking to release the AC inmates who were least likely to become involved in racial conflicts in order to free up the space.

After a lengthy discussion, Jacobs agreed to the release of Passaro, and I put the word out for the Angels to meet with me. When three of them showed up, I told them I was going to release Passaro back to the general population.

"But I'm going to hold you to your word of good behavior on the part of all involved parties," I reminded them. The three assured me again there would be no problems. Later, as Passaro walked out of the AC front door, a group of fellow Hells Angels greeted him with hugs and good-natured back slapping.

From that day on, I never heard another word about Passaro as long as both he and I were at San Quentin. The Hells Angels had stayed true to their word. And in August 1971, I would learn how much Passaro's release meant to them.

CHAPTER ELEVEN

THE PERFECT STORM

In 1970 I was still working as the lieutenant in charge of the Lockup at San Quentin. It was indeed a tumultuous time to be a law enforcement officer. The destructive racial unrest between blacks and whites in America was overshadowing the peaceful efforts for civil rights and equality. After the assassinations of Martin Luther King, Jr. and Robert F. Kennedy in 1968, the words and actions of militant, revolutionary members of extremist groups became louder and more volatile. Peaceful protests just weren't cutting it for them anymore. And their hostility toward government, law enforcement, and other forms of authority was influential.

Impatient radical groups began splintering off the revolutionary momentum. The Black Panthers, formed by Huey Newton and Bobby Seale in 1966 in Oakland, California, and the Weather Underground, formed in 1969 mainly in opposition to the Vietnam War, were joining forces and pushing their aggressive declaration of war against "the establishment."

Because the cultural twists and turns in a free society eventually make their way over prison walls, I found myself experiencing an undercurrent of apprehension within the Lockup. I had the dreaded feeling of some impending disaster bubbling just under the surface in my AC housing unit. If I had poked my head out the door I was sure I would see a full moon.

I initially waved it away as a consequence of the large number of radical dissidents who were housed there at the time. But the feeling seemed to take on weight and hang in the air like the stench that can rise out of a cell block full of sweaty men in the middle of summer. My fellow officers were also starting to get the same uneasy feeling, a sixth sense that tells you something's just not right.

Call it a heightened awareness – of where we work, the job we do, and the sometimes eerie nuances that can raise the hair on the back of your neck as you walk down the tier in a maximum security cell block. When night has fallen and inmates have ceased talking to each other from cell to cell, the tier is dead quiet. That is sometimes as unsettling as the noise level during an all-out insurrection. Silence can be downright spooky in a prison. But when there's an extraordinary amount of noise on the tier, you have to wonder if someone got hold of some tools and is busy cutting away at his cell bars while the other inmates keep the tier boisterous to mask the sound.

"The key is to be prepared for anything and trust your instincts," I advised new officers. "Don't ever underestimate your good old intuition – especially when it's as bothersome as a toothache." And mine was.

The escalating racial tension wasn't exclusive to San Quentin. In early July 1970, we received three inmates from Soledad Prison. They were John Clutchette, Fleeta Drumgo, and George Jackson – all members of the Black Panthers. The three had been transferred to San Quentin to await trial in the January killing of a white Soledad correctional officer – a retaliation killing if ever there was one.

On January 13, 1970, Officer Opie Miller stood armed with a rifle on a gun tower high above an exercise yard at Soledad Prison. It was a routine assignment for Miller, an expert marksman. Though the assignment was routine, the event wasn't. Sixteen inmates – fourteen black and two white – were released onto the recreation yard. They were all maximum security convicts. It was the first integrated exercise period in several months, as the institution had been experiencing an increase in racial conflict. Miller stood ready for any violence that might erupt among the high-security prisoners. Minutes later, the inmates were clumped together on the yard fighting to the death with clenched fists and brute strength. Certain that several inmates could be hurt or killed in the brawl, Officer Miller blew his whistle and fired his rifle. His intent was to disable them and stop the melee. The gunfire injured one white inmate and killed three black inmates.

Three days after the January 13 incident, a twenty-six-year-old white correctional officer named John V. Mills entered the maximum security Y Wing. The inmates were listening to a news report from the Monterey County district attorney regarding Officer Miller's actions on January 13. The DA determined the officer did his job as trained and with due diligence. He was a gunpost officer whose job was to stop inmate fights on the yard. The investigation found no punishable offense. Miller would not be prosecuted.

Many prisoners believed a line had been drawn in the sand when Officer Miller, a white man, fired on the group of inmates, killing three, all of them black. When the Monterey County Grand Jury exonerated him, it was all the inmates needed to justify their next move.

John Mills, a husband and father, was the only officer in the room at the time the exoneration was reported. Less than a half hour later he lay dying on the floor of the cell block. He was attacked by a group of incensed inmates and severely beaten. Hell bent on revenge and making a statement that wouldn't soon be forgotten, they dragged a battered Mills up three flights of stairs and threw him over the tier railing to his death.

Inmates Clutchette, Drumgo, and Jackson were responsible for Officer Mills' death, according to inmate eyewitnesses. The three were charged with the killing. In a show of support, other prisoners dubbed Clutchette, Drumgo, and Jackson the Soledad Brothers, giving them a moniker of hero status that followed them from prison cells to courtrooms to newspaper headlines.

Jackson's attorneys and many of his supporters denied the suggestion that Mills' killing was in retaliation for the deaths of the three black inmates days earlier. But a note reportedly left beside Mills' badly beaten corpse was strong evidence to back that theory. It read simply, "One down, two to go."

About six months later, on July 23, 1970, another white officer, William H. Shull, a forty-year-old father of four, was found dead in a prison shed at Soledad. He'd been beaten and stabbed more than forty times with a metal file that had been sharpened into a shank – a precise killing weapon. Two officers brutally murdered in the line of duty in six months. Two down, one to go?

In August 1970, James McClain, another San Quentin AC inmate, was being tried in Marin County for a 1969 non-lethal stabbing assault on San Quentin Officer E.K. Erwin. The attack on Officer Erwin took place in a dining hall while he was supervising the inmates passing through the chow line to receive their meals. Not exactly a time you'd expect a bloody attack, but I learned long ago not to underestimate the criminal mind.

On August 7, San Quentin was under court order to have inmate McClain and two inmate witnesses appear in Judge Haley's Marin County Superior Court for McClain's trial. George Jackson was supposed to be a witness for McClain on that day, but at the last minute his appearance was rescheduled for another day. The court had ordered that only a maximum of two San Quentin inmate witnesses could be present in the courtroom at any given time. The two inmate witnesses called that day were William Christmas and Ruchell Magee.

George Jackson's teenage brother, Jonathan Jackson, had devised a plan to free the Soledad Brothers – including his brother, George – during a hostage siege in Marin County Superior Court. Thinking his brother would be one of the witnesses in court that day, Jonathan arrived at the Marin County Hall of Justice with a grandiose scheme up his sleeve – and a sawed-off shotgun and two other weapons concealed inside his long raincoat. Despite the fact that it wasn't at all raincoat weather, Jonathan strode into the courtroom with all the daring of a seasoned criminal at least twice his age. No one was the wiser as the heavily armed Jackson blended into the crowd.

The weapons Jonathan carried were registered to Angela Davis, at the time a known radical political activist and leader in the Communist Party USA. She was also known by some as George Jackson's pen pal and love interest.

Seated in the courtroom were several San Quentin officers who had escorted the prisoners to court that day. Under direct orders from Judge Haley, all were unarmed. But two armed court bailiffs were also there – one in the judge's docket area and the other in the spectator section.

A few minutes into the trial, the young Jackson pulled two weapons from their dark hiding place inside his raincoat. He threw one pistol to the defendant McClain and with one word took control of the courtroom. *"Freeze!"* Jackson yelled. Within minutes, McClain, Christmas, Magee, and Jackson had taken Judge Haley, the deputy district attorney, and three others hostage.

The incident was playing out like a star-studded gangster movie. With weapons drawn and guiding their way, the abductors moved the hostages out of the courthouse and into a rented van. They'd planned to drive to the airport for a swift and safe exit on a hijacked aircraft. By this time, numerous law enforcement agencies had descended on the scene outside the Hall of Justice. For extra insurance against interruption, Jackson's sawed-off shotgun had been crudely taped to Judge Haley's chest, the gun barrel perched just under his chin. With Haley's life held in delicate balance, the group made an easy unobstructed getaway out of the building, past waiting authorities and the press.

Meanwhile, not far from there, Correctional Sergeant John Matthews had five new correctional officers at the San Quentin rifle range for training. Matthews, a certified firearms instructor, was certifying the rookies under California Penal Code 832 – the mandatory Arrest and Firearms Course for all peace officers.

Upon hearing of the escape attempt at the courthouse over his radio, Sergeant Matthews immediately loaded the officers into a prison vehicle and drove to the Marin County Civic Center, just a few miles from the prison. They set up a perimeter on the street leading from the courthouse at the Civic Center Hall of Justice and waited.

The van carrying the hostages was driven by Jonathan Jackson. From a van window, inmate McClain fired at law enforcement as they sped through the parking lot in a rush for freedom. As the getaway van passed Matthews and his officers, Jackson fired his pistol at him from the driver's side window. Matthews returned fire and the shooter went down as the van came to a stop. Just then, another escapee appeared in the window and fired one shot at Matthews and his officers. He returned fire and the shooter went down. A few seconds later, a third shot was fired from the van, and Matthews again returned fire. Then everything went silent.

Because California's Corrections Department policy does not recognize a hostage as a bargaining tool in an escape attempt, lethal methods of resolution are permitted and expected. Sometimes it's the only way to thwart an escape attempt and keep dangerous armed criminals from disappearing into the community.

When the dramatic incident was over, the van was littered with bodies and blood. Jonathan Jackson was dead. So too were inmates Christmas and McClain. During the shootout, the shotgun taped to Judge Haley went off, killing him instantly. The deputy district attorney was shot and permanently paralyzed. A juror hostage suffered a bullet wound to her arm. Inmate witness Magee was injured in the gun battle, and later pleaded guilty to aggravated kidnapping. He was sentenced to life in prison.

Back at San Quentin, Warden Nelson held a debriefing following the incident. In the meeting he told Sergeant Matthews and his recruits they had done exactly what was expected of them – prevent an escape. He reassured the officers that using force was the proper thing to do in that situation.

"We will hear nothing but criticism about this," he told them. The media was typically not supportive of use-of-force issues. "I want to reassure you that I'm behind you one hundred percent. Our job is to protect the public from escaping convicts, and we are empowered to use any force necessary – including lethal," Warden Nelson stated. "I will always back you on that. The law will back you on that, too."

The bold plan of young Jonathan Jackson to free the Soledad Brothers was reduced to bloodshed in the streets – and his death at age seventeen. An arrest warrant was issued for Angela Davis for her part in the purchase of the weapons used in the crime. She fled the area and eluded authorities until October 1970, when the FBI found her in New York City. Davis was charged and tried as an accomplice to conspiracy, kidnapping, and homicide. She was acquitted on all counts.

◆

At San Quentin, inmate assaults and yard fights were becoming frequent, sometimes more than a dozen incidents a week, including several attacks on officers. Between January 13, 1970, and January 16, 1970, more than three dozen California prison inmates were assaulted by other inmates. Three dozen in three days. The wheels of violence were shifting into overdrive.

At 11 p.m. one night in March 1971, Correctional Officer Robert McCarthy was working the head count in X-Wing at Soledad Prison. An inmate called him over to his cell saying he had a letter he wanted mailed out the next day. When McCarthy got close to the cell front, the convict stabbed the forty-three-year-old father of two in the neck, killing him.

The inmate was Hugo 'Yogi' Pinell – a particularly evil member of the Black Guerrilla Family prison gang. He was serving time on a rape conviction, and was also awaiting charges of assaulting an officer in December 1970. He killed McCarthy with a sharpened pencil.

A couple of months later, in May 1971, Soledad Prison racked up its ninth killing in eighteen months when Kenneth Conant was murdered in his office. The forty-nine-year-old program administrator was stabbed in the back of the head with an inmate-manufactured knife.

When Conant was killed, I started to worry more than I wanted to. I felt more attacks were coming, and I began to think about the places that seemed ripe for a breach of security. We were classifying inmates in a small room at the time. Classifying is done to determine an inmate's housing and program needs. The process decides the inmate's custody status. In that room, the inmate would appear before a committee of about four officers and a warden or associate warden.

The conditions in the classifying room were just a little too close for comfort, if you ask me – especially as assaults seemed to be on the increase. It would be so easy in that cramped little room to really do some damage. When an inmate entered the room, his body literally blocked the door – the only exit. If he was armed with a knife, it could mean significant injury or death to one or more officers before the convict could be restrained. They are that fast and that determined.

With the old rumor mill churning about inmates wanting to kill more officers, the administration should have taken more precautions. The Conant killing stoked the flames of apprehension inside those walls. And no one tried to put out the fire.

In the months leading up to the summer of 1971, racial tension was very high out on the streets, and protests over the Vietnam War, then in its sixteenth year, weren't going away. The free speech movement in Berkeley, the growing gang influence, and the escalating rhetoric of the Black Panther Party, whose leaders advocated for violent action, began to merge as one revolutionary voice against war and oppression. Radicalized sympathizers of all causes were rethinking peaceful protests in favor of more disruptive activism. Clearly, a swelling wave of rebellion was rolling in.

My anxiety level took its cue from that active rumor mill. Images of an all-out riot flashed before my mind's eye, and I tried to design an orderly and swift end in my head. I began to talk more frequently about riots and other emergencies in our routine safety meetings. I told my staff we'd storm the cell block with weapons if necessary to stop an insurrection and restore order – *before sundown*. Heinze's managerial directive kept popping up in my head like an offshore distress signal.

Other nuances of impending disaster began to appear. Incoming inmate mail was scrutinized more carefully for any messages that appeared to be coded or particularly disturbing. The prison outgoing mail had increased dramatically. The mailroom sergeant should have monitored this change and passed it along to the higher-ups. He may have and his superiors simply didn't feel the same sense of urgency that we were feeling.

Inmates began using thick monthly magazines as body armor. They strategically tucked them underneath their clothing to appear more muscular and threatening to the other inmates, as well as for some protection during knife attacks on the yard.

Convict *chatter* was also on the rise at this time. In prison, there's always an underlying element of espionage whispered about the cell blocks and exercise yards. This chatter can range from grandstanding threats of violence and prison takeovers to valid warnings from worried cell mates.

A few of us began to keep notes of unusual or troubling comments the inmates made, sometimes under their breath and with a sinister smirk. It was no easy task picking through the typical hateful rhetoric to find the genuine clues of some nefarious plot. Like looking for the proverbial needle in a haystack, we sifted through ample colorful language for something more telling than the usual demeaning comments about our mothers and their sex lives.

Officers learn to tune out most of the juvenile and bullying remarks as they go about their duties. But some messages from inmates can be hard to ignore. George Jackson's whispered warning, "The dragon will rise," during routine searches was just such a comment. We didn't legitimize a statement like that by responding to it, though we made mental notes of it for good reason. That sort of remark can be as startling as a loud knock on your front door in the middle of the night. It merits some attention.

◆

Even more disturbing, in the weeks leading up to August 21, some of the convicts' attorneys were pestering officials about the visiting process, which they claimed left something to be desired. Unwarranted complaints of a lack of confidentiality, a crowded visiting area, or long wait times for visiting rooms clouded the administration's thinking, prompting an unnecessary and dangerous reevaluation of the long-standing policy.

In 1971, the visitation rules stated that inmates could only have ten approved visitors on their visiting card kept on file. Only one of those could be a friend, the other nine had to be relatives. In order for a friend to be approved for this list, he or she had to be a long-standing friend of the inmate.

All visitors were required to walk through a metal detector before entering the prison's visitation waiting room to stem the flow of contraband into the facility. Visitors setting off the metal detector were denied entrance to maintain the integrity of the institution. Women wearing underwire bras might set off the detector; large metal buttons and fasteners on clothing items could also set off the alarm. Purses were not allowed in the Visitor Center – only plastic see-through coin pouches to hold money for the vending machines. All other personal items had to be kept in the visitors' vehicles in the parking lot. Attorney briefcases with metallic locks that could set off the detector were hand-searched by an officer.

Associate Warden James Park was the liberal voice to Warden Nelson's conservative enforcement style. I'm sure the warden thought he and Park created a good balance. Maybe they did, at times. But I always questioned Park's ability to truly comprehend the rebellious capacity of some convicts. He had a tendency to only see the good side of people, which is commendable. But in a maximum security cell block, a one-sided view of inmates can get you into trouble fast. Some of those people simply don't have a good side, and that must be considered when dealing with that kind of element. Many of them have no intention of turning their lives around and leaving a life of crime in the wake. Of the several thousand convicted murderers I came to know over my long career, I'd need only one hand to count the ones who eventually gave up their criminal ways.

But Park always wanted to be seen as the good guy. In the summer of 1971, he finally yielded to the attorneys' unrelenting requests for a different visiting environment. Park authorized an alarming change in the visiting procedure. He allowed the attorneys to come into the Adjustment Center itself, inside the maximum security Lockup, to visit with their clients. The controversial move didn't sit well with me and many other officers. His decision unnerved me, to say the least.

"Oh, this is not a good move at all," I told a few fellow officers when we got wind of the policy change. Several of us were already wary of the motivations of some of the attorneys who visited on a regular basis, and we weren't about to be snowed by their claims of an inadequate visiting environment. Deep down, I knew there was nothing wrong with the visiting procedure.

My guess was the attorneys sensed that Park was sympathetic to their task and jumped on it. I didn't trust their intentions for a minute. I was afraid their persistent nagging was simply a way for them to get into the Adjustment Center – one step closer to the inmates and an easier route to smuggling in drugs or something worse. When Park gave in to the grumbling legal reps, I could almost feel the institution tremble in anticipation of what was to come.

But my hands were tied. All I could do was take my objections – and those of my coworkers – to my direct contact, Associate Warden Jacobs. I could always count on him to keep a level head and strongly share his unwavering common sense in staff meetings. But the team of Park and Warden Nelson ultimately made the final decision and that was that. The administration eventually moved the attorney visits to the second floor of the AC in one of several small offices in a row. Instead of regular walls, the offices featured security glass between the rooms.

I had an office about two rooms down from where the attorneys would be sitting with their inmate clients. During one of their first visits in this new arrangement, I sat down in my office and went about my day, completing paperwork and other tasks.

Knowing I was in plain view because of the glass walls, I nonchalantly put on a set of headphones, letting the cord dangle down toward the floor as if it were plugged into a recording device. I sat there, staring straight ahead pretending to listen intently to something or someone through the headphones. I knew they could see me sitting there from their visiting room, and I knew they had no idea that my headphones were just a prop.

That turned out to be the last time the attorneys used that room. My guess is they thought it was bugged. That was exactly the impression I wanted to give them. My law enforcement intuition told me Park's visiting room change was a big mistake, and I was determined to discourage it. *If you see something, do something.*

◆

By the summer of 1971, I was the correctional lieutenant in charge of the Lockup and the B Section of the South Block – the other maximum security housing unit on the property. B Section had 250 cells that could temporarily house the non-compliant bad guys of general population. I had a well-trained staff of about 150 officers and sergeants to manage the 24-hour, day-to-day operation of these two max-security cell blocks.

Racial tension was a growing problem inside the prison. Staff were getting assaulted on a regular basis, and the violence between black inmates and white inmates was escalating. In one year leading up to August 1971, there were twenty stabbings at San Quentin.

Sergeant B.J. Kennedy remembered the months leading into the summer of 1971 as particularly violent. One day, working the night watch in B Section, he got an uneasy feeling about the way some of the inmates were behaving. He told a fellow officer, "You're not going up on that tier today. I'm not sure exactly why but I don't think it's safe." When the day shift came on, during breakfast feeding, he told another sergeant that an inmate assigned to the serving crew had been acting strangely. "He needs to be taken off the serving crew," Kennedy told him. The other sergeant didn't heed the advice.

"Later that day I heard a stabbing had taken place in B Section," Kennedy recently told me. "That inmate who was acting up had stabbed an officer."

◆

"There's something wrong here," I said out of the blue one day to another officer. We were sitting in the yard office and I was looking toward the Lockup unit. When the officer barely mumbled an acknowledgement, I offered an explanation.

"I've got a hunch that one of these days we're going to have to retake that Adjustment Center with machine guns." He was a veteran officer, but the look on his face told me he didn't put much stock in my warning. Maybe he thought I was being melodramatic. I decided to silently sort through the strange feeling.

I'd been thinking about the hints of potential trouble that were floating all around us. Call them warning signs or red flags, they told us what we needed to know. But the prison wasn't getting the message.

The August 1 incident when Jackson's visitors tested the prison's response to a fake gun hiding beneath a child's pant leg should have raised more suspicion than it did.

Shortly after that incident, another red flag appeared and dramatically waved itself right under our noses. The eternally combative Hugo Pinell had been escorted from the Visitor Center back to his cell in the Lockup. I was on the tier observing as he went through the routine unclothed body search just inside the AC entrance. Officer Mike Loftin was the escorting officer.

Standing there at arms reach from Pinell, Loftin and I were unarmed and unprepared for what happened next. After the search, Pinell calmly and slowly got dressed. When his last button was fastened, he suddenly lunged at us in a violent flash. With a grunt that summoned an amazing burst of strength, he grabbed both me *and* Officer Loftin in a bear hug and pulled us down the corridor. We fought hard to defend ourselves, but were unable to combat his extreme body strength. On any given day, Pinell was in great physical shape. His biceps were huge and as solid as boulders. But on this day he seemed to have the power of three grown men, reinforced by an extraordinary amount of rage. He moved the two of us as easily as dragging pillows down a hallway.

"Hit the alarm! Hit the alarm!" I yelled over and over again to anyone within earshot. The alarm switch is in a red electrical box above the main door to the AC. This switch activates a loud buzzer on the outside of the Adjustment Center building, alerting staff that help is needed immediately inside the unit.

As Loftin and I struggled to get free from Pinell, he muscled us into the sergeant's office and then into a small staff restroom. With another grunt, he shoved Loftin to the ground and hoisted me above the toilet, standing me up in the john like he was jamming a stick into the dirt. My shoes and socks were soaked in toilet water. In that instant, responding officers arrived to help.

As they burst into the room, Pinell's attack suspiciously stopped as abruptly as it had begun. He showed no resistance to responding staff. Pinell simply dropped his assault as if he were filming a scene in a movie and the director had yelled "Cut!"

It was a risky move on his part. Attacking staff is a serious offense, punishable by added time on a sentence or extra time in the Lockup. Worse, Pinell's attack had all the earmarks of a trial run to gauge the response of officers to the incident. And it was likely not a solo run. I had a very strong hunch that a co-conspirator had to be timing the response from the safety of a locked cell down the tier.

Collectively, all these odd hints indicated some unidentifiable trouble was on the way. I was certain of it. All the signs were there. A menacing storm was bearing down. And the Lockup at San Quentin was directly in its path.

CHAPTER TWELVE

A CLEAR AND PRESENT DANGER

Outside the walls of San Quentin, the nationwide Civil Rights movement fanned the flames of freedom fighters doing time. The Black Panther chapter inside San Quentin was bolstered by the support of radical advocates on the outside. It was led primarily by inmate George Jackson, who preached violence and "death to the pigs" as a way to effect social change. The chapter seemed determined to foment the racial divide and rise up against authority.

Over the last four decades, there have been many interpretations of the restless and dangerous George Lester Jackson. Countless newspaper articles, editorials, essays, books, websites and documentaries have been written and produced about Jackson's struggles with race issues, oppression, and a reluctance to follow the law.

Though he grew up in a low income neighborhood, Jackson was the product of a middle class family. His father was a postal worker, his mother described as God-fearing and strong-willed. Though he attended a private Catholic elementary school, he was no stranger to trouble. Jackson was a small-time criminal from Chicago who had regular run-ins with the law before he was ten years of age. A family move to Southern California when Jackson was a teen didn't have the desired effect on George's delinquent ways that his anxious father likely was hoping for.

As a teen in Los Angeles, Jackson did time in California's youth correctional facilities for various crimes, including armed robbery, assault, and burglary. His first major crime involved a small heist at a gas station, which netted the nineteen-year-old about seventy dollars and a one-year-to-life prison sentence. His many prior offenses didn't help his case.

In prison, Jackson's long-held dislike for law enforcement thrived. Along with other extremist inmates, he studied the works of radical political theorists Karl Marx, Mao Tse Tung, and others. Those prison study groups eventually became the Black Guerrilla Family, the revolutionary prison gang that still exists today.

In his own published letters and essays, which were many and lengthy, Jackson's continual condemnation of law enforcement as "pigs," and his repeated threats of a "grand revolution" revealed a career criminal who took little if any accountability for his actions. He was a narcissistic thug who though aware of his own imperfections, was unwilling to address them. Instead, he chose to hinge all of his miseries on others – especially those in authority. In May 1970, Jackson stated his position in a letter to fellow rebel Angela Davis:

"I don't believe in mercy or forgiveness or restraint. I've gone to great lengths to learn every dirty trick devised and have improvised some new ones of my own. I don't play fair, don't fight fair. As I think of this present situation, the things that happen all day, the case they've saddled me with, no one will profit from this, sister. They created this situation. All that flows from it is their responsibility. They've created in me one irate, resentful nigger and it's building – to what climax?"

The twenty-nine-year-old Jackson had been transferred to San Quentin when Officer Mills' murder trial venue was moved from Monterey County to San Francisco County. He was classified as a maximum security prisoner, and was housed on the first floor of the Lockup under my supervision.

Inside San Quentin, Jackson surrounded himself with "yes" men, which amounted to nothing more than an adoration society to feed his growing ego. He never quite rose to the level that his ego had crafted for him, but the delusions of grandeur that fueled his mission got him a handful of faithful followers in prison and a flock of sympathetic supporters on the outside.

"George Jackson became a *cause celebre* to the leftists," former San Quentin C.O. Daniel P. Scarborough wrote in his book. "He had a great number of visitors, from the elite to the low-lifes, from the legitimate press to the leftist press."

Jackson's high-profile supporters included Angela Davis, anti-war activist Tom Hayden, actress Jane Fonda, and prominent New York attorney William Kunstler, who later acted as a negotiator for the inmates during the deadly uprising and hostage siege at Attica Correctional Facility in September 1971.

Former Chief Psychiatrist Frank Rundle, who handled all the Lockup cases at Soledad Prison in those days, observed that many followers of Jackson had put it into his head that he was some sort of hero, building the great fantasy of Jackson's revolutionary dragon. By the time he got to San Quentin, Jackson was fully engulfed in the role of egotistical hero, taunting officers as he collected supportive fans inside and outside prison walls like groupies on tour with a rock band.

"He worked himself into this larger-than-life persona," recalled Sergeant Kennedy, who noted Jackson rarely slept lying down on his bunk." He'd move the mattress up the wall a bit, and slept sitting up on his bunk facing the cell front," Kennedy explained. "And day or night, anytime you walked down that tier and past his cell, he was watching you."

The George Jackson I knew – and I knew him pretty well – was hardly the beloved redeemer he thought he was. Though he had devoted followers, he was an intimidating bully who hustled weaker, more subservient inmates for everything from coffee to toilet paper. I wouldn't be surprised to learn he regularly stole lunch money from grade school chums back in the day.

My conversations with Jackson mainly took place when he was either going to or returning from a visit, or while he was being searched. We never exchanged normal day-to-day dialogue, such as "Pretty cold out there today," or "Who do you like in the Super Bowl," as officers did — still do — with many of the inmates. Though they're convicted felons, these are people the officers see day after day, at least five days a week, sometimes for many years. Brief conversations will naturally occur.

But exchanges with Jackson were typically centered around Jackson. His words were delivered on a cloud of innuendo, the kind of quiet, assured bravado of a man who thought he held all the secrets. We'd exchange our civil *Hellos*, and then he'd start in with how great he was, how powerful his revolution was going to be, and the support of his many followers. He wasn't as intelligent as he probably thought he was, though he wasn't stupid either. He was definitely a survivor in the prison culture, able to uphold the jailhouse image he had drawn for himself. That takes a measurable amount of both book smarts and street smarts.

Jackson was never going to be capable of small talk with the officers he encountered as he went in and out of the AC every day. As a rule, inmates who are filled with hate or consistently deny any responsibility for their situation simply aren't interested in our predictions of who might take the World Series that year. Jackson was a known cop hater with a chip on his shoulder. We weren't going to be pals.

But small talk isn't the only way to get to know inmates. Watching their behavior as they interact with other inmates in the cell block or on the yard can offer a fairly clear picture of a man's character – or lack thereof.

Jackson was "an unscrupulous bully," according to the late John Irwin, a former Soledad inmate turned college professor and prisoners' advocate. Though many of his fellow inmates believed in the theories Jackson shared in his writings, they didn't care much for the guy behind them. As Irwin has described, he was in many ways "a self-serving, aggressive asshole."

Jackson was a dangerous man who had many faces. He could be charismatic one minute, wicked the next. Though many people around the country were peacefully marching for civil rights at this time in our history, Jackson elevated it to an all-out war of blacks vs. whites and of George vs. the rest of the world. He hated authority, and yet he lived his life in a manner that would put him in front of it many times in his short lifespan. He admonished others for what he saw as a lackluster passion to fight against oppression in the more demonstrative way in which he was. He held to the belief that the black race would win this war of color he had declared. In fact, it was his goal.

Jackson's letters in his book *Soledad Brother* paint a revealing self-portrait of the kind of man he was. Though his writings have been criticized by some as not entirely his own words, they do align with the persona Jackson created and displayed in prison.

"My credo is to seize the pig by the tusks and ride him till his neck breaks. But if fortuitous outcome of circumstance allows him to prevail over me – again – then I want to have this carefully worked-up comment prepared. I want something to remain, to torment his ass, to haunt him, to make him know in no uncertain terms that he did incur this nigger's sore disfavor."

◆

On July 21, 1971, a black inmate who claimed to have witnessed Jackson and John Clutchette brutally kill Officer Mills at Soledad was being housed in a cell in San Quentin's prison hospital. Normally, he would have been housed in the Lockup prior to trial. But due to the Black Panther sympathizers residing at the time in the AC, the witness was instead housed in the hospital for his own safety. Officer Leo Davis was assigned to stand guard outside the inmate's hospital cell, further ensuring his safety before the trial.

Officer Davis was an unassuming kind of guy who never gravitated toward workplace drama. In fact, he was a very likable coworker. On July 21, he was filling in for another officer.

I was working in B Section of the South Block unit when the hospital alarm went off about noon. Hearing the alarm, Sergeant Joe Rose and I bolted up and took off running.

"Second floor! Second floor!" the staff frantically directed as we burst through the front door of the four-story hospital building. We ran up the stairs to the second floor where staff told us to head down the center corridor.

Sergeant Kennedy was working as a relief sergeant one day a week in the prison hospital. "Get down and lock this place down!" he immediately told staff when the alarm went off. He and another officer started down the hall and around the corner, where they saw Officer Davis lying on the floor. He tried to speak but couldn't. Shaking, he gingerly slipped off his wrist watch and handed it to Kennedy. Likely fearing he might not survive, he passed on the watch to a friendly face so that it could quickly be returned to his family in the event of his death.

Sergeant Kennedy retraced the officer's steps back to where Davis had been giving round-the-clock protection to the inmate witness. His chair was overturned, and the blood on the wall and the floor told of the gruesome assault that had happened only seconds earlier. The attacker was nowhere in sight.

As Sergeant Rose and I neared the end of the corridor, I saw Officer Davis on the floor, lying on his side. I ran over to him and knelt down, touching his arm lightly. His eyes were closed and he had lost all color in his face.

"Leo! Can you hear me, Leo?" I asked him, studying his face for a flicker of recognition. He was bleeding from the mouth and his body twitched from the severity of the attack. Each tremor further soaked his uniform in blood through stab wounds I couldn't see. I heard death trying its best to rattle up from his limp body. I watched helplessly as my friend and coworker desperately clung to life. Within seconds, responding medical staff arrived, placed Officer Davis on a gurney, and rushed him down the hall into the hospital's surgery unit.

Sergeant Rose hoisted an oak desk chair high above his head and smashed it to the floor with a crashing thud! He grabbed one of the sheared-off legs to use as a weapon. Davis's attacker was still in the hospital somewhere, we thought, and except for the jagged-edged chair leg we were unarmed. Rose followed the trail of Davis' blood on the polished hallway floor to the end of the north corridor, where I caught up with him. There, we turned left to run up the west corridor, still following the trail of blood. Davis had traveled more than eighty feet before he collapsed after the brutal assault. The inmate he was guarding was unharmed.

There wasn't a soul in sight so I returned to the surgery area. The prison-wide alarm had not been sounded so I dialed 9 on the hospital phone, which goes immediately to the prison operator as an emergency call. From where I stood, I could see into the surgery unit where staff were attempting to resuscitate my friend Leo. A few minutes later, the chief medical officer walked out of the surgery unit, looked my way, and slowly shook his head. Davis had succumbed to his injuries. Just that quickly we lost a decent officer in the line of duty. Davis was a thirty-eight-year-old husband and father of four. He was a good man who quietly did his job, and ended up paying the ultimate price. He gave his life to save an inmate's life. Though widely understood as a fundamental risk of the job, it's never easy to accept. It's even harder to witness.

Naturally, a lengthy investigation began in the hospital, so I remained in the area to assist the Marin County Sheriff's Department and other investigators.

Davis' killer had ducked into an unlocked, empty cell at the end of the hallway. The murder weapon, an inmate-manufactured shank, had been thrown out the window of the cell and was later found on a courtyard rooftop. The cell contained bloody clothing, indicating the killer had cleaned up after murdering Davis, wiping his blood from his hands, before casually leaving the cell sometime later when he would not be observed by staff.

Fortunately, Davis' killer never got to the inmate witness tucked safely away in the hospital cell because the prison's protective order included an added level of security. Davis could never have opened the cell on command as his attacker surely demanded, because he simply didn't have the key. Whenever the inmate witness was to be moved either in or out of the cell, another officer in the building would have to bring the key to the cell each time to ensure two officers participated in the cell opening. Tragically, when the attacker realized Davis could not open the cell alone, he must have known his plan to kill the inmate witness was failing. Surely, he'd be subject to disciplinary action. Possibly out of ruthless disgust at the system, or maybe just pure hatred, the attacker decided to kill the one witness in front of him – Officer Davis.

What the killer didn't know was that another inmate in a cell next to the one being guarded by Davis had witnessed his murder. As I probed the crime scene for clues, checking the floor for bits of evidence, the inmate quietly called out to me from his cell.

"Nelson, c'mere, c'mere. I know all about this attack," he whispered. I knew this inmate well. He'd been a reliable informant in the past. There was no reason to doubt him now.

"I wanna talk to the investigator," he added as I walked toward the cell. "I wanna tell him what happened."

Officer Davis had been ambushed and brutally killed in the hospital hallway by Larry Justice and Earl Gibson, two Black Panther inmates who were determined to permanently silence the inmate Davis was guarding. But the witness had survived to give his testimony in court. And the other inmate who witnessed the killing of Officer Davis gave his testimony at the trial of Justice and Gibson. To ensure his safety from retaliation, the informant was subsequently relocated to another correctional institution.

Justice and Gibson were found guilty of Davis' murder. However, their convictions were reversed on appeal and the district attorney declined to retry the case due to a lack of evidence for a solid conviction. Though they escaped conviction on the murder charge, the two were charged on a Corrections 115 infraction, a rule violation report that mandates an administrative hearing rather than a courtroom hearing. The U.S. Supreme Court long ago determined a convict could be found innocent in a court of law and still be found guilty of a departmental 115 violation, where the burden of proof for a guilty verdict is lower. Justice and Gibson, found guilty of the 115 infraction, were eventually moved to the Lockup.

My nagging hunches began poking at my brain for attention. Many of us weren't convinced the trouble was all over with after Officer Davis was killed. There's always a possibility of more trouble. And there had been a lot of stabbings in a short period of time. Theories of revenge dangled in front of us like a carrot on a stick, daring us to make the connections and circle the wagons.

When it all finally came to a head, a period of about thirty minutes on the 21st day of August 1971 proved to be a catastrophic event of such magnitude that it would change Corrections in California for good. In a flash on that Saturday afternoon, six lives would end, young families would be devastated, and a profession would be shaken to its core. Here's how the dreadful day played out.

CHAPTER THIRTEEN

A DRAGON RISES

Reluctantly, I had decided to back-burner my persistent desire to go fishing and instead use my day off to repaint our dining room. I flung open the windows and picked up my paint brush. I was hoping for a breeze off the Bay to drop the temperature as much as to whip the paint fumes out of the small room. I once heard that stirring a little bit of vanilla extract into a can of paint will do away with paint fumes. That might be great while you're doing the painting but what if the sweet aroma lingered? I wasn't so sure I'd want the smell of cupcakes to outgun my Thanksgiving turkey, so I nixed the vanilla idea and trudged along.

In the middle of my painting project, I walked out to the backyard to get a breath of fresh air. Standing on the back patio, I rubbed at the dried yellow paint specks on my hands. Suddenly, I heard what sounded like a muffled pistol shot. The sound of gunfire can mean big trouble in a prison setting, as guns are not allowed inside a facility, except on elevated gun posts. Even the slightest chance that a convict might get his hands on an officer's gun is reason enough to keep weapons off the ground – except in response to emergencies.

When I heard the shot, I quickly ran around to the front of the house to get a better view down into the prison. I strained to hear any other sounds that might fill in the details of what was happening inside those walls. From that vantage point, I could see the yard office near the Adjustment Center, the roof of the chapel, and the roadway behind the chapel that leads from the lower yard to the upper yard. I didn't see anything out of the ordinary – no one running from one building to another responding to alarms or cries for help, no inmates on the loose fighting or running for freedom.

But I definitely noticed the prison's visual alarm system.

San Quentin's emergency notification consisted of three lights on a tower above North Block's Death Row: a green light, which was almost always on, indicating everything was OK at the prison; a solid red light that when lit meant something was not right inside, such as a bad count and a missing inmate but the situation was under control. But a rotating flashing red light meant a dire emergency was taking place. All hands on deck. In our household, if the light was flashing red, our kids knew to get inside the house pronto, pull the shades, and lock the doors to keep a desperate inmate on the run from turning our home into a hideout.

My daughter had instinctively followed me outside the house. When that pistol went off she came to alert like a bird dog! Our children were no strangers to the unique sights and sounds of a prison, and the older ones knew what to look for in an emergency and how to respond. Standing next to me on the lawn, Jill's eyes widened in shock and she pointed to the flashing beacon as if it were a monster coming straight at us. She ran back into the house without a sound.

I waited and listened. Straining to get a better view, I looked down into the prison. Just then two loud, distinctive rifle shots broke the quiet surrounding my front lawn. First one – *CRACK!* Then several seconds later another – *CRACK!* A pistol being fired is a sort of muted sound, while a rifle shot will shatter the air with an explosive sound similar to smacking two large bricks together. I couldn't place exactly where the shots came from but I knew it had to be off a gunwalk inside the prison. Two houses up the street, Associate Warden James Park had also run out onto his front lawn at the sound of gunfire.

"There's trouble inside! We better get in there!" he frantically hollered. I was already running back into my house.

Even before I bolted for the front door, my mind had begun its own race. Instinctively, I knew that all available officers would be needed inside that prison if we were going to stop the rampage that was finally taking place.

But something else propelled me toward the danger. Another force stronger than intuition firmly placed its hands on my back and pushed. I was the lieutenant in charge of the AC – where I was betting the trouble began. That area was my responsibility, an obligation I took very seriously. The inmates residing in the AC and the officers working there were under my supervision. I felt an extremely strong sense of duty to get in there and right whatever wrongs were taking place. All of my senses stood at attention and every muscle awaited my marching orders. I knew what needed to be done and I knew just how to do it.

Moving as quickly as possible, I changed from my splotched painter's pants into my Corrections uniform. In a situation like this, where the first instinct is to simply run down the hill into the thick of it, I knew I'd never be allowed inside the gate to help out unless I was in uniform. Because I lived on the prison grounds and was in charge of the Lockup, I was on call twenty-four hours a day. I always kept a spare clean, pressed uniform at the ready.

As I dressed, the phone rang. Prison operator Wayne 'Woody' Woodside reported a convict armed with a gun had rushed into the prison chapel. Even before Woody said the inmate's name, I knew who he was talking about. But it instantly raised the hair on the back of my neck as it confirmed my suspicions.

George Jackson's dislike for law enforcement was by now well known throughout the institution. And for months he'd been taunting staff with his hints at an insurrection. The dragon was rising, just as promised. Jackson was finally making good on his threats of a grand revolution. In a max-security cell block, quiet order can change to deadly chaos in the blink of an eye. My gut told me to expect the worst.

"Jackson's got a gun and he's loose in the prison!" I blurted out to Shirley as I hung up the phone. I turned toward her just in time to see her face fall and the color drain from her usually rosy cheeks. My wife was a strong and resolute woman, and her stoic German heritage always held her together – at least in my presence. She may have fallen apart when I walked out the door but she rarely showed fear to me or the kids. The second the words were out of my mouth I regretted saying them.

As I threw on my uniform, Shirley sprung into action rounding up our children and securing the homestead. We'd been married for more than a decade, and Shirley's role as family matriarch was much like mine as a state correctional officer: heavily steeped in tradition and dedication. I was sworn to protect the public by maintaining the security of the institution. Shirley was bound by that almighty maternal instinct to protect our children as much as she could in the face of a terrifying situation unfolding less than three hundred yards from our home.

As I rushed out of the house, I knew this day would be different from all the rest. I may have known exactly where I was going but I sure as hell didn't know where I was going to end up. I left my family to worry and wait inside the spacious master bathroom upstairs where they had the best overall view of the prison's main entrance and lawn. The large bay window looked out over the prison chapel roof and right up to the Adjustment Center entrance.

Our four-year-old, Debbie, was lying on the living room couch when the sound of the pistol pierced the air. She ran to the window and saw the bright-red beacon.

"Mom! Mom! The gumball machine is flashing!" she shrieked. At that announcement, Shirley calmly enlisted the help of Debbie and Jill in immediately locking all the windows and doors that had until that moment spent the day wide open, trying to coax a cool breeze in off the Bay.

Jeff, three, was too young to fully understand what was happening. But he followed Mom and his sisters to the upstairs bathroom where they all watched as scenes of a prison riot played out like a horror film viewed from the front row of the theater. As the drama unfolded, Shirley and the kids could see and hear the arriving ambulances and local law enforcement vehicles speeding along the prison road. Their screeching sirens cut through the air like a knife. On occasion, our oldest, twelve-year-old Kim, would get scared when I went into emergency mode and rushed into work to help with prison uprisings or locate missing inmates. Though it was rare, she occasionally saw her mother break down in tears out of fear for my safety. And Kim was old enough to understand when Shirley would muster all her strength to compose herself so as not to frighten the younger ones.

◆

Sprinting toward the armory to get a weapon, I had only one thought: do whatever it takes to stop Jackson. If he had one weapon, he surely could have more than that – and ample ammunition as well. I ran faster down the hill about a block and a half and burst into the armory.

The information I didn't have weighed heavier on my mind than the few facts I did know. Was Jackson acting alone? How did he get out of the Lockup? How many weapons did he have? How much ammunition? Though I still didn't know just what we were up against, I knew I could be successful with the firepower of a machine gun.

I first learned to use a field machine gun in ROTC in 1955 with a 1917 water-cooled, 30-caliber weapon from the first World War.

It wasn't a stretch to think I would need that kind of weaponry on this day. I grabbed one of my favorites: a 1920s 45-caliber Thompson sub-machine gun. Good old dependable Mr. Thompson, as I liked to call it. Most people preferred the slang Tommy gun, or its original name, the Annihilator. Its rate of fire was reported to be nearly eight hundred rounds per minute.

As a law enforcement officer I was a qualified sharpshooter with a rifle and a marksman with a pistol, but I was an expert with a machine gun. Even without knowing exactly what I'd be walking into, I was fairly certain whatever firepower Jackson had would be no match against Mr. Thompson. And I couldn't see him going down without a fight. *Fairly* certain would have to do.

"Bill! Check me out on the Thompson!" I called out as I sprinted from the armory with my weapon and a couple of clips of ammunition. Officer William Twells was manning the inside gate of the double-gated front entrance, a position usually staffed by an inmate *except* during an emergency. Though I was confident of my skills with the Thompson, it had been a few months since I'd fired one. I wanted another experienced officer to be a second set of eyes on the weapon. Twells was it. He was a friendly guy with the kind of slow-drawl voice of someone who didn't know the definition of stress. Though his personality could fool you into thinking he was somewhat lackadaisical, he was a seasoned serious officer who knew his stuff.

Aware of the grave situation and my urgency, Twells took the weapon in hand and carefully but quickly looked it over to make sure it was ready for action. Counting off the elements out loud, he checked the trigger pull, safety switch, full automatic, all of it before thrusting it back into my hands, "Y'er good! Go!"

Lieutenant Mike Luxford was at the AC entrance when he noticed me running toward the chapel where I thought Jackson was armed and lying in wait.

Luxford was working as relief lieutenant on my day off. Like me, he was an avid fisherman. We were about the same age so we became good fishing buddies in no time. We worked out a great partnership. He had a real nice boat, so I bought the fuel and we'd spend hours out on the Bay catching our limit of salmon.

"Dick, over here!" They have hostages!" Luxford yelled at me.

"Jackson's loose in the chapel with a gun!" I yelled back, still running.

"Jackson's been shot behind the chapel!" he corrected me. "Get over here quick! They have weapons and hostages!"

I made an abrupt left turn and ran toward the AC. Weapons *and* hostages? I'm always surprised by how many thoughts can pop up in my brain in a split second. In the time it took me to run thirty yards, my mind started to form images of what could be going on inside that max-security unit. Based on the tone in Luxford's voice and the overall dark cloud of urgency that hung low over the institution at that moment, it felt like the whole world knew something we didn't.

Entering the Adjustment Center, I was immediately hit with the stench of spilled blood – a lot of blood. It smelled metallic and almost sweet as it formed puddles on the cold concrete floor. Grotesque, bright red pools, some a half-inch deep, marked the spots where grave injuries began and lives ended. The heat inside the building also held an odor of vomit and feces in the air, telling us how victims reacted to their assaults. I couldn't see the attacks going on in the cells, but the remnants of rage were all around us.

"Oh, Jesus . . . " I barely whispered. The cell doors of violent prisoners were wide open, the cells empty. The thought made my skin crawl. Clothing, sheets, and mattresses stained with blood had been flung out of cells in obvious fits of fury. "Kill the pigs!" and other hateful threats came at us from the back of the tier like a swarm of angry wasps on a charge.

As my senses surveyed the area, I quickly tried to think who might have been working this shift. But the odor, the sights, and the sounds inside that cell block were almost paralyzing. What vile hell had erupted here?

CHAPTER FOURTEEN

THE DEVIL'S DEN

Officer B.C. Betts had been manning the Inspectoscope Gate outside the prison's Visitor Center during an extremely busy Saturday morning. Groups of visitors seemed to come in waves between the facility's routine gate traffic – the milk truck, the outside patrol vehicles, and the medical staff.

All potential visitors had to successfully pass through the metal detector before being allowed entrance to the visiting area. During Betts' shift, approximately ten people had to go back through the beeping metal detector a second time to make sure they were contraband-free. One fellow tripped the alarm with a metal apparatus around his ankle that attached to a medical brace inside his shoe. Before that, a young girl's Naugahyde coat kept her from getting a clean reading. She removed the thick coat and walked through the gate with no problem. Betts shook the coat thoroughly and checked the hems and pocket linings for any contraband. He finally determined the coat's large metal buttons were setting off the alarm.

Sometime before 10:30 a.m., a petite and smartly dressed Vanita Anderson approached the gate requesting a visit with inmate George Jackson. She was carrying a large briefcase.

"What is your title or position?" Officer Betts asked, glancing down at her briefcase.

"I'm a legal investigator." Her icy reply was accompanied by a glare of contempt. Curt, even snippy responses were no surprise to officers working the Visitor Center. Many of the inmate attorneys and legal reps had an obvious disdain for officers. Their loyalties were with the felons they represented. To them, officers were the bad guys.

At Betts' request, the woman passed her briefcase over to the officer for inspection but not before she made sure he had seen the scowl on her face. Betts was careful to strategically place the item on the pavement so it would still be in plain view of the visitor.

Anderson walked through the metal detector with no problem. Knowing the metal adornments on the case would set off the alarm like an armful of military weapons, Betts carefully carried the briefcase over to the desk and opened it, spreading the sides wide to view down into the dark opening. The satchel was about half full with legal papers and a small tape recorder, approximately five or six inches wide and ten inches long.

Dutifully, Betts fully examined the tape recorder for contraband. He looked at the face of the recorder, turned it over and opened up the back, revealing several batteries, a speaker, the basic insides of a recording machine. Satisfied, he put it back together and returned it to Anderson. She walked up the pathway toward the visitor's waiting room about fifty yards away.

Officer Daniel Scarborough was working the busy front desk. Saturdays in the visiting area can resemble a big city subway terminal. Fathers, mothers, wives, and children mingled alongside inmate attorneys and their special investigators carrying bulging, accordion-style legal folders and leather briefcases.

Inside the waiting room, twenty-nine-year-old attorney Stephen Mitchell Bingham was also there to see Jackson. Along with fellow Soledad Brothers John Clutchette and Fleeta Drumgo, Jackson was scheduled for court in San Francisco on Monday, August. 23 for the killing of Officer Mills in 1970.

Between his family and his legal issues Jackson was in and out of the visiting area nearly every day it was open. Family members, lawyers, and legal assistants visited him on a regular basis. I'd estimate he had nearly seventy visits in less than ninety days in the summer of 1971.

Contrary to popular myth, Jackson was not in solitary confinement. Because of the bar design of the cells in those days, he was easily able to communicate with other inmates in cells on either side of him. In addition, we had special exercise yards for the AC inmates. Jackson was assigned a yard, but I don't recall ever seeing him go into that yard. He opted instead to work out in his cell doing pushups, pullups, and other calisthenics. Virtually all of his out-of-cell activity was in a visiting room.

Bingham greeted Anderson, and the two approached Officer Scarborough at the front desk. Bingham was a tall lanky New Englander from a wealthy family in Connecticut. But he didn't look the part. His unkempt hair and clothing certainly didn't match the image of a well-to-do attorney. After a stint in the Peace Corps and degrees from Yale University and the University of California at Berkeley, Bingham settled in on the West Coast, joining a law collective as a civil rights attorney.

Legal investigators are only allowed one visit per week, and Anderson had already visited Jackson earlier that week. Scarborough denied her request to visit on this Saturday. According to Jackson's file, Bingham was not Jackson's attorney of record and therefore had no legal right to visit with Jackson. And there was no required letter on file from Jackson giving Bingham permission to visit him in a legal capacity. Therefore, Scarborough denied his request as well. The two visitors weren't happy with those decisions. Bingham asked to see someone with more authority.

Anderson and Bingham argued their case with Lieutenant Robert Milloy. They claimed to have permission from Associate Warden Park to visit Jackson. However, no required written authorization to back up that claim could be found in Jackson's file. Bingham also insisted Jackson's regular attorney, John Thorne, had contacted Associate Warden Park to get Bingham permission to visit Jackson. Again, no letter of authorization existed to back that claim. Following policy, Lieutenant Milloy supported Officer Scarborough's decision and told the would-be visitors the answer was still *no*.

Bingham was again unsatisfied. He demanded to see Associate Warden Park immediately. Since it was a Saturday, Park was not in his office. Looking around the busy room, Scarborough decided he'd had enough of this radical troublemaker. He told Bingham if he wanted to get permission to visit he'd have to contact Park himself. Milloy agreed to allow Bingham to visit with Jackson if he got approval from Park.

Warden Louis Nelson was on vacation at the time, and Park was the acting warden for the day. Though Park wasn't on site when Bingham and Anderson were trying to visit, he was expected back soon. Bingham elected to wait it out. Even though she wouldn't be allowed to visit, Anderson also took a seat in the waiting room. Shortly before his shift ended at 11 a.m., Lieutenant Milloy called the East Gate officer and instructed him to have Park contact the Visitor Center as soon as he returned to the institution.

◆

Inside the Adjustment Center, Sergeant Ken McCray and Officers Paul Krasenes and Urbano 'Rubi' Rubiaco were supervising the first floor.

At my request, McCray had been recently assigned as the relief sergeant in the Lockup. He and I had worked together at Folsom, where we formed a good working relationship. McCray was a very likable guy with a strong work ethic. He was not one of those *office* sergeants. He kept busy all day, moving about the tiers, checking on the inmates working housekeeping tasks, or just walking and talking with the inmates. He spoke fluent Spanish and was highly respected by many of the Mexican inmates. He transferred in to San Quentin a couple of years before me.

"I got a visit and you guys ain't givin' it to me," Jackson called out repeatedly from his cell. He'd been pestering staff throughout the morning about the visit he was expecting that day. He was outwardly anxious that he might not get his visit on this Saturday. Rubiaco, who was filling in for another officer who wanted the day off to attend a friend's wedding, called the Visitor Center inquiring about his visitors, and each time Rubiaco was told there was, so far, no approved visitor for Jackson.

In addition, the Visitor Center staff were repeatedly bothered that morning by other inmates, including Hugo Pinell, the aggressive inmate who had shoved my feet into the toilet, questioning the delayed arrival of Jackson's visitors. That's behavior that should raise suspicion. It's uncommon for inmates to inquire about the visitors of other inmates.

Finally, Scarborough received a phone call from Associate Warden Park. He had spoken to Bingham during one of the attorney's many calls made that morning from the telephone booth inside the Visitor Center. Park approved Bingham's visit with Jackson.

Carrying his large legal folder and Anderson's tape recorder, Bingham went into visiting room A, and the door was locked behind him. There, he waited for Jackson.

Prior to his escort to the visiting area, Jackson was skin-searched by Officer Rubiaco and Sergeant McCray in the Lockup. Jackson exited his cell and walked to the grill gate at the front of the tier. He removed his clothing, passing his pants, shirt, underwear, socks, and shoes through the bars to Rubiaco and McCray, who thoroughly checked the clothing for contraband.

McCray checked Jackson's pants, each leg and hem, and gave his shoes a once-over. Standing next to McCray, Rubiaco gave Jackson's shirt and underwear a good shaking before running his fingers over the shirt's sleeves and hem to check for any hidden items.

While his clothes were searched, Jackson casually walked back up the tier. Talking with a couple of inmates through the bars of their cells, he used a comb to fluff out his typically unfluffed Afro. Pulling the comb through it to pump up the volume, Jackson primped and groomed himself as he stood naked waiting for his clothes. Must be an important visit, Rubiaco thought.

Standing at the gate, McCray told Jackson to run his fingers through his hair for a final search to show there was nothing hiding in it. It's still part of the search procedure even if an inmate has just been seen grooming his hair. Cleared, Jackson dressed and was escorted across the yard to the Visitor Center.

Sergeant Jimmie Cry and Officer E. L. Osborne were working Condemned Row on the third floor of the Adjustment Center. Osborne happened to glance out the window just as a yard officer was escorting Jackson from the AC.

"Wow, Jackson's got his hair fluffed out more than usual today," Osborne said to the sergeant, who was also standing near the window.

"Yeah, I noticed that, too."

◆

In the visiting room, Bingham and Jackson were seated across from one another at the small wooden table. For some reason, the steel mesh grate designed to prevent smuggling was not utilized during this visit. I'd guess Park relaxed orders for the security grates in visiting rooms A and B, likely under pressure from inmate attorneys.

In an odd twist during their visit, Bingham requested to leave the visiting room for a few minutes. As is policy, an officer first escorted Jackson from the room, and he waited in the passage way. Bingham left the room and took a seat in the large waiting room next to Anderson. He returned a few minutes later. Jackson was escorted back to the room and their visit resumed.

An hour or so later, officers working in the Visitor Center were preparing to close up for the day. Inmates heading back to their cells were given the usual search before leaving the area. Jackson had concluded his visit with his attorney and was escorted out of the room before Bingham was allowed to leave. Following procedure, a Visitor Center officer administered a clothed-body, pat-down search of Jackson before he left the building. Officer Frank DeLeon was detailed to escort Jackson back to his cell in the Lockup.

Forty-four-year-old DeLeon, a U.S. military veteran with a strong square jaw and a haircut to match, was in his fourth year as a correctional officer. He and Jackson arrived at the entrance to the AC. Because the door is always locked, the escorting officer must use his keys to gain entrance.

When Officer DeLeon entered the Lockup just behind Jackson, McCray, Rubiaco and Krasenes were in the control corridor foyer. Jackson walked over to a side table to disrobe for his routine search before heading back to his cell. DeLeon recorded Jackson's return time at 2:27 p.m. in the Adjustment Center register.

All seemed routine. But Jackson held a secret. The Visitor Center staff and escorting officer were unaware that Jackson had left the visiting area wearing an Afro-style wig. Somehow during his visit with Bingham, Jackson secretly slipped on a wig. It closely resembled his own hair color and style, particularly on this day, so no one noticed anything out of the ordinary. Well, almost no one.

Jackson placed his large legal envelopes on the table. He undid first one, then another button on his regulation dark blue denim shirt. Before he could go any further, Rubiaco stopped him.

"What've you got there?" Rubi asked Jackson, pointing to a tiny glint of something poking out of his hair. Jackson didn't say a word.

Rubiaco was a tall husky Philipino with dark hair and a baby face. Easily one of the most trustworthy people I've ever worked with, Rubiaco was the kind of officer any prison supervisor would want under his wing. He was knowledgable, hardworking, and committed to the solid security of the institution.

"Stand still a minute," Rubi said, tilting his head to get a better look. His ample height gave him an advantage. Reaching out, he lightly touched the end of a metallic object slightly visible in Jackson's hair. Sergeant McCray stood nearby, observing the search. Rubiaco took a step back and directed Jackson to fluff his hair with his fingers.

At Rubiaco's order, Jackson lightly rubbed his fingers over the top of his hair, as if to show him he had nothing to hide. Just then McCray also noticed something peeking out of the thick black hair.

"OK, Jackson, let's have it," McCray demanded, instructing him to give up whatever he was hiding.

Jackson was cornered. Rubiaco, Krasenes, DeLeon and McCray looked on, waiting for Jackson to do as told. Instead, he took a couple of steps backward, yanked the wig off and pulled out a semi-automatic 9mm pistol. Simultaneously, a clip of ammunition fell to the ground. Rubiaco instinctively started to reach for it. Jackson slammed another clip into the butt of the gun with a defiant shove and aimed it at Rubiaco's head.

"Freeze!" Jackson ordered triumphantly. Pointing the weapon at the four officers standing in the corridor, he added boldly, "This is it, gentlemen. The dragon has come."

In that split second, Jackson was now the one in charge of the Lockup. He had made it back from the Visitor Center with a deadly weapon and two clips of ammo tucked under a contraband wig.

Jackson obviously meant to get back to his cell with the goods. Was he going to use the weapon during his court appearance on Monday, taking advantage of a day off prison grounds to escape? Maybe. But Rubiaco's keen eye threw a monkey wrench into his strategy. This may not have been Jackson's Plan A, but he didn't let the glitch stop his revolution from moving forward. With the weapon now discovered, he was forced to resort to Plan B – a sudden and deadly rewrite that he made up on the spot.

"Get down on the floor, face down, and stay there!" Jackson told the four officers as he retrieved the clip on the floor. The officers had no good option. Outside the Lockup, it was business as usual. Staff went about their duties in the yard office, the Visitor Center, and the other cell blocks. At this moment in time, nobody else on the property had any idea of the monster that was rearing up on the first floor of the max-security Lockup. The officers complied with Jackson's demand.

"You, throw the bars!" Jackson waved his weapon at Rubiaco, ordering him to open all the cell doors. Rubiaco moved slowly, horrified at the thought of the ruthless and dangerous men in those cells suddenly being on the loose. Noticing his hesitation, Jackson maintained his composure as he threatened Rubiaco. "Either you do it or I'll shoot these pigs in front of you and then I'll shoot you."

Rubiaco walked over to the steel control box on the wall. What in the world could Jackson be planning with this move, Rubiaco wondered. What level of evil does it take to knowingly release the treacherous individuals housed here?

Though there are thirty-four cells on the first floor, seventeen on each side of the tier, only twenty-six were occupied that day.

The AC's remote-control locking system consists of one locking/unlocking lever for each cell, and one similar lever marked A for *ALL*. This one lever could open all seventeen cells down the tier on one side simultaneously. To open one cell door, a lever marked with the cell number is flipped and a hand crank is used to roll the door open. Officer Rubiaco was obviously fully aware of the system. Jackson and the other inmates were not.

With no regard for his own safety should Jackson suddenly figure out the mechanics, Rubi began to slowly open the cell doors. Hoping to stall Jackson's reign of terror he opened one cell at a time instead of seventeen cells at once. The clicking sound of their cells unlocking must have startled some of the inmates who were unaware at that moment of what was happening at the front of the tier.

Rubiaco turned the hand crank to slide each heavy cell door wide open. You'd think century-old metal would significantly creak as it rolled round and round, but it didn't. Consistent maintenance kept the locking system in tip-top shape. Every two months or so every lock on every cell door would be completely exposed, examined, and greased up till it glistened.

As their cell doors rolled open signaling freedom, the inmates walked out. Some were cautious at first. Most were undoubtedly curious. Standing behind Rubiaco, Jackson set the scene for his fellow inmates.

"I got caught off guard," Jackson hinted at a foiled plot and the very real possibility that at least some of them knew of his plan. "We all gotta do it together. We gotta do this now or never!" The inmates responded by gathering at the front of the tier.

Still lying on the floor, McCray noticed inmates Johnny Spain and Hugo Pinell come out of their cells and rush toward their leader in the foyer. Armed with a convict's version of riot gear — crudely manufactured weapons, torn sheets, pillow cases, and radio earphone cords — they came for battle. The weapon of choice: shortened toothbrushes with razor blade tips imbedded in the ends.

Because these weapons were small and short, making them difficult to handle in thrusting stabbing motions, the killing would have to be modified. Attackers would slash an officer's throat with the makeshift weapon, then go in for the jugular vein with a sharpened pencil or nail clippers, digging and poking at the vulnerable lifeline. If they could puncture it, the officer would bleed to death before help could arrive. It's an extremely raw and desperate act.

Pinell quickly used an earphone cord to tie McCray's feet and hands behind him. The inmates then dragged him down the north side of the tier, stopping just in front of Jackson's cell, 1-AC-6. One of them threw something – a shirt or sheet – over McCray's head.

All around him, inmates were coming out of their cells and running to the front of the tier, eager to join in the revolution. Fleeta Drumgo joined his fellow Soledad Brother and leader in the improvised uprising. As he walked past Officer Krasenes lying on the floor, Drumgo kicked him square in the face. Rubiaco instinctively lunged at the inmate.

"You make a move like that again, it's gonna be your last!" Jackson warned him. Grimly, Rubi continued opening the cells.

Holding Officer McCray down on the floor with a foot on his back, an inmate lifted his head and used a crude weapon to slit his throat from ear to ear. Blood instantly gushed from the gaping wound as McCray's skin gave way as easily as torn tissue paper. His blood turned his neck into a river, soaking his uniform shirt. It was relatively painless and swift, confirming the fact that it was likely a sharp razor blade cut.

The instant it happened, McCray went limp, hoping to feign death. Given the level of the injury, it couldn't have been a difficult effort. He was then dragged into the cell and thrown face down in the corner like a sack of dirty laundry. On his way out of the cell, an inmate ripped McCray's set of keys from his uniform.

Left to bleed to death, McCray didn't dare move or make a sound. If he turned his head to see what was happening on the tier, the inmates might notice he was still alive. He could only listen as the mayhem took place all around him.

Minutes later, Officer Krasenes was dragged into the same cell. The inmates had tied his feet and hands behind him with torn bedsheets. He was beaten, slashed, and strangled with an earphone cord before being tossed to the floor and left for dead. Unfortunately, his body was so traumatized by the attack that he began to cough and vomit.

"This one's still alive!" McCray heard someone yell. Then he heard a struggle, and Krasenes desperately gasping for air. "May God have mercy on my soul," were the final words of the husband and father just months away from retirement. The inmates dropped his body on top of McCray.

Though he couldn't see all of the attackers, McCray heard familiar voices. Pinell, Jackson, and Luis Talamantez, a known ruthless gang member, were right in the thick of it. The savagery and strength of rioting inmates is a brute force like no other. As their level of violence escalated from victim to victim, the cruelty of their acts intensified.

Officer DeLeon was also bound, slashed, and beaten. The inmates forced him into the cell that now resembled a human slaughterhouse. Finally, as his attackers began to choke him with a cord, he pleaded for his life.

"For God's sake, don't kill me! I've got five kids!" DeLeon struggled to get the words out, trying desperately to stay alive.

"You have to twist harder," Talamantez told Pinell in Spanish.

The cell went silent as DeLeon's last efforts were surrendered.

The small space had become a grisly torture chamber and makeshift morgue. The battered officers were thrown on top of each other like raw slabs of beef in a butcher's freezer. A woeful scent of death began to rise out of that cell block. The revolutionaries were taking over the tier, systematically killing or attempting to kill anyone who stood in their way.

As McCray lay motionless, blood filled his mouth from his slashed throat. Although the weight of his coworkers on top of him was nearly suffocating, it put enough pressure on his neck to close his wound somewhat and keep him alive.

◆

Jackson's other Soledad Brother, John Clutchette, had visited with a family member in visiting room B that afternoon. When the Visitor Center started closing up for the day, Officer Chad Breckenridge was dispatched to escort Clutchette back to his cell in the Lockup.

When they approached the AC entrance, Clutchette rang the outside bell and Rubiaco came to the door. As he opened it, Jackson was crouched down in hiding. Suddenly he stood up, revealing the gun in his hand.

"Be quiet and get inside," Jackson waved the weapon at Breckenridge.

A young man in his mid-twenties, Breckenridge was average height with a slight build. He was gifted the nickname Hippie by fellow officers because he wore those wire-rimmed "John Lennon" eyeglasses. His personality fit the style, as he was known for being a laid-back, peaceful officer.

As he stepped into the AC corridor, Breckenridge noticed inmate Pinell walking out of the sergeant's office carrying a pen knife.

"Keep walking over to the south side," Pinell told Breckenridge. Walking behind the officer, Pinell took on the role of second in command. "Put 'em in sixty-three," he told a couple of inmates, who walked Breckenridge and Rubiaco down the tier.

Breckenridge was forced into cell 1-AC-63, pushed from behind face first onto the bunk. Inmates David Johnson and Willie Tate tied his hands and feet behind him with torn pieces of cloth. Rubiaco was forced into the same cell and also shoved onto the bunk, causing Breckenridge to slip halfway off of it. His upper body was still on the bunk, his knees resting on the floor.

The inmates used Rubi's own set of handcuffs to restrain his hands behind his back, and hogtied them to his feet with torn bedsheets. Breckenridge heard Pinell's voice behind him and knew by the sound in that cell that his fellow officer was being tortured. Out of the corner of his eye, Rubiaco saw fingernail clippers in an inmate's hand. He was quickly stabbed on the side of the neck, his attacker then using the clippers to dig inside his wound, looking to damage the jugular vein and bring swift death.

An inmate outside the cell called out, "Make sure they're dead!" Someone grabbed Rubiaco's forehead from behind, lifting his head and neck backward. Leaning in to Rubi's ear, the inmate said, "I love pigs" before slashing his throat from ear to ear.

"Don't do it, Yogi!" Breckenridge recognized Pinell's voice. "There's no need for this."

"Shut up! You don't know who this is!" Pinell responded in anger. Breckenridge was stabbed twice in the throat from behind.

The inmates left the cell all at once, but returned almost immediately. They untied Breckenridge's hands and removed his uniform shirt before hastily rebinding his hands.

Outside cell sixty-three, Breckenridge and Rubiaco heard the usual sounds of rioting maximum security prisoners. Vile threats blew through the tier like howling storm winds as the rioters darted back and forth past the open cell.

"Hey, these pigs in here aren't dead yet!" Breckenridge heard Tate yell.

"Go in and strangle 'em!" Pinell ordered. Inmate Johnson came into the cell and placed a torn strip of bedsheet around

Breckenridge's neck, pulling it tighter and tighter. Again, he was stabbed in the throat. As Breckenridge struggled to get oxygen, convicts untied his ankles, removed his uniform boots and pants, and retied his feet together. By now his torso was fully blanketed in his blood.

As life literally dripped out of the officers, an inmate jumped on Rubiaco's back. Trying to smother him, the inmate forced his face into the growing puddle of blood. Rubi held his breath as long as he could. Finally, his attacker stopped. Unsure if he had left the cell, Rubi kept his eyes closed and tried to remain as still as fallen snow, hoping to appear dead. His neck wounds were throbbing, the tight handcuffs cutting into the skin on his wrists.

The inmates left the cell again, leaving the officers to wonder if they'd bleed to death before the inmates came back to finish the job.

◆

Outside the Lockup, Yard Sergeant Jere Graham was wondering what could be taking his escort officers so long. It had been ten minutes or more since DeLeon and Breckenridge escorted Jackson and Clutchette back to the AC. They should have returned to their other duties by now. He decided to investigate.

A phone call to Officer Carl Adams, who was working in the yard office opposite the entrance to the Lockup, confirmed that the two officers escorted the inmates back into the AC within minutes of each other. But neither officer had been observed coming back out of the building.

"Well, I'm coming down there," said Graham, who was working on this Saturday so another officer could start his vacation early. "I want you to let me into the Lockup so I can see what the heck they're doing."

When they approached the AC entrance, Adams and Graham looked in through the door's window and saw no movement. No officers or inmates in the corridor, nothing out of the ordinary. Adams unlocked the door, Graham walked inside, and Adams closed the door behind him.

Jackson suddenly appeared in the door's window. Thinking Adams had locked the door, he waved his gun at him, "Open this goddamn door or I'll blow your head off!"

Adams immediately ducked down as far as he could. Jackson fired his weapon through the window but missed his target. The yard office was about twenty yards away. Officer Adams took off.

"Hit the alarm!" he hollered as he ran. "They're bustin' out of the AC!" he yelled to another officer as he dove into the yard office and called for help on the intercom.

A minute earlier, on the third floor of the Lockup, Officer Osborne had a hunch something wasn't right. He walked over to the window to survey the yard office and plaza area outside the AC building.

"Something's happening downstairs," he said to Sergeant Cry. The jolting explosion of Jackson's gunfire proved his suspicion midsentence as it rattled the floor beneath them. The officers immediately secured the floor by locking their side of the outer door.

On the second floor, Officer Bill Hampton was sitting in his office with Sergeant John Kentzel. Officers Gerald Riley and D.L. Johnson had just finished distributing meals and medications. At the sound of the gunfire, they jumped into action.

"Get down there and see if you can help out!" the sergeant told the officers. Johnson and Hampton rushed immediately to the first floor. At the bottom of the stairs, Officer Johnson looked through the window in the door.

"Look out, everybody's out!" he cautioned Hampton. Figuring staff needed help with brawling inmates, they started through the doorway. Right away, Hampton noticed the security grill gates for both sides of the tier were open. Inmates were trafficking in and out of the north and south sides of the tier and in the corridor. Not at all an ordinary scene for the max-security Lockup. What's worse, he couldn't see one officer in the area.

Suddenly inmate Spain appeared in front of Hampton. "Hold it right there!" Spain said, pointing a revolver at the officer. Inmate Tate picked up a bucket full of garbage, threatening to throw it at the officers. "You better get the hell outta here!" he warned them.

Hampton immediately backed up through the doorway and locked it. He and Johnson rushed back up to the second floor, locked up the entrance, and informed the sergeant of what they found on the first floor.

Worried the rioting inmates might easily get their hands on a set of keys, Sergeant Kentzel directed Johnson and Hampton to firmly hold their key inside the door lock so no one could insert another key on the outer lock and gain entry to the second floor. The officers then used serving tables and other furniture to barricade the door. Kentzel collected all other keys from his staff and hid them in the unit. If their floor was somehow raided, the inmates wouldn't be able to get access to other areas – including the condemned inmates on the third floor.

The sergeant passed out batons, a can of mace, and tear gas billy clubs to the three officers. There they waited, securing themselves, the inmates, and other staff on floors two and three. They waited for a break-in, for an assault, for the siege to be over.

◆

Once inside the Lockup, Sergeant Graham was quickly grabbed by inmates, his hands and feet bound like the others. He was stabbed in the chest and abdomen. Jackson pushed him into the cell with the other victims, shoving him onto the bunk.

"It's time I see how good this piece really works," Jackson threatened Graham, aiming the gun at the officer.

"Good God, man, no!" Graham cried out. Jackson shot him point blank in the head. Sitting on the bunk, he slumped against the wall.

CHAPTER FIFTEEN

INTO HARM'S WAY

After supervising the noon meal in B Section, Lieutenant Luxford was walking back toward the yard office when he heard Officer Adams yell out, "Inmates with guns in the Lockup trying to break out!"

Luxford was directly adjacent to the AC wall at that moment, and noticed officers on the gunwalk of the North Block housing unit proceeding down toward the AC.

"Get back! Get back!" he shouted. "Cover the area but use the North Block wall as a shield in case armed inmates come out of the AC!"

By now, nearly everyone at the prison had heard the pistol shots in the Lockup and were on emergency alert. Officers arriving at the gate to come on duty knew immediately of the grave situation when they saw the flashing red beacon. All available officers were hitting the armory in droves, grabbing weapons, and rushing to spots north, south, east, and west to secure the institution.

The gunwalks and balconies were filling up with officers armed to the teeth to stop any fleeing inmates – and to keep a steady eye on the entrance to the Lockup. It was certain a security breach had occurred, but no one knew for sure what was taking place inside the max-security cell block.

As Luxford stepped into the yard office, inmates Jackson and Spain suddenly flew out of the AC at a full run. A handful of rioting inmates stood just inside the doorway, possibly trying to decide if they, too, should make a run for it.

As Jackson and Spain ran past the yard office, Luxford noticed a pistol in Jackson's hand. The escapees headed toward the chapel and the roadway leading down the hill to the lower yard. A balcony gunpost officer above them yelled "Halt!" Still running, Jackson turned and took a potshot at him. The officer fired back at Jackson, hitting him in the ankle. The impact pitched him forward but didn't stop him. He briefly stumbled but quickly recovered. Doubled over, he continued to run.

An officer on the North Block gunwalk heard the shots the same time he heard someone yell "Inmate with a pistol!" The officer ran to a corner of the gunwalk, dropped to a prone position, and carefully aimed his weapon.

As Jackson rounded the corner of the chapel, the officer fired one round. Because Jackson was bent over, the bullet hit him at the base of the spine, traveled up his spinal column, and exited through the top of his skull. He dropped dead on the pathway beside the chapel. Blood drained out of Jackson's head and pooled in the dirt next to his body.

◆

Lieutenant Eugene Ziemer was in the snack bar when the emergency call came through. The Adjustment Center was under siege. He immediately ordered all personnel in the snack bar to go to the armory for weapons. A rugged, decorated U.S. Navy war hero from Colorado, Ziemer was a conservative, rock-solid custody man who didn't take any crap from the inmates. If they spoke to him respectfully, he reciprocated. If they were disrespectful, he reciprocated.

Once armed, some officers were dispatched to the chapel plaza, while others were told to give gun coverage at the rear of the Adjustment Center. Ziemer then ordered four officers to get in a vehicle and cover the area immediately outside the chapel in the event of an escape attempt.

As the lieutenant rushed toward the AC, he noticed Officer Adams pulling an inmate from the bushes near the chapel. Johnny Spain, who had run from the Lockup with Jackson, dove into the bushes for cover when the first balcony officer fired his weapon.

Ziemer ran across the patio to offer assistance, but Adams had subdued Spain. It was then he noticed Jackson lying face down on the roadway next to them. Ziemer bent down, grabbed his body by the shoulder, and turned him over on his back. When he did, the gun slid out of Jackson's hand. His arms lay outstretched on the dirt roadway, his legs crossed at the ankles.

Searching Jackson's body and the area around it, Ziemer discovered a clip containing eight 9mm cartridges and a metal safety clip that had broken off the weapon when Jackson fell to the ground.

Lieutenant Bill Sellmer heard the gunshots from the visitor parking lot and rushed through the gate toward the chapel garden. He summoned five armed officers and directed them to serve as additional security to the outside perimeter. Neither Lieutenant Ziemer nor Officer Adams had a set of handcuffs, which wasn't out of the ordinary for the times, so Sellmer ran to the yard office to retrieve a pair. After cuffing inmate Spain, Lieutenants Sellmer and Ziemer headed to join the many officers who were running toward harm's way in the Adjustment Center. Though Jackson was dead and his accomplice in restraints, the ordeal was far from over. Jackson was only the tip of the iceberg.

Jackson's bolt for freedom had left the entrance door to the Lockup wide open. Inside the yard office, Luxford's phone calls to the AC went unanswered. He knew there had been officers inside the AC before Jackson ran out. But who? How many? And were they still alive? He cautioned unarmed officers to stay down in case there were additional armed inmates inside the max-security unit. Watching intently, Luxford waited for any sign of movement near the Lockup.

Like me, Lieutenants Sellmer and Stewart both lived on the prison grounds. Sellmer, the son of a Marin County sheriff's deputy, was very knowledgeable about custody detail. He was consistently supportive of the uniformed staff and was well-respected at San Quentin where he spent his entire Corrections career.

Lieutenant Al Stewart was a small guy with a sharp tongue. Though he was a bit of a shit-talker, he was a solid supervisory influence with a lot of experience to back him up. He just happened to be coming through the East Gate when Jackson kicked off his revolution. Seeing officers running in the plaza, hearing their shouted warnings, he ran straight to the armory.

◆

Ziemer was one of the first to arrive on the scene inside the Lockup. He entered cautiously. From the sound of things, he knew the rioting inmates had sequestered themselves on the south side of the tier, farthest from the entrance. But from the look of things, he knew hostages were dead or dying in Jackson's cell on the north side.

Armed with a tear gas billy club, and with several armed officers covering his back at the front of the tier, Ziemer started down the north side. He walked slowly past cells one, two, and three, peering into each cell until he came upon the grisly mess in cell number six. It looked as if someone had thrown open cans of red paint all over the inside of the cell.

Inmate John Lynn was lying on the floor halfway out of the cell. He tried unsuccessfully to speak. Near death, he'd been slashed and tortured like the officers. He wouldn't survive the attack.

Then Ziemer recognized four officers, bloodied, battered, and lifeless. Three were piled together on the floor, face down, their heads toward the back of the cell. Sergeant Graham was on the bunk. Looking closer, Ziemer noticed movement from underneath the bodies of Krasenes and DeLeon. Sergeant McCray had heard the voices of responding officers. Though weakened by his injury, he found the strength to call out to Ziemer.

"Get these bodies off me . . . I'm drowning in the blood!"

"Get a gurney in here fast! McCray's still alive!" Ziemer shouted. He and other responders began pulling the bodies of the dead officers out of the cell. Lifting and moving the deceased officers proved difficult given the amount of blood covering the floor. It was so thick that a firm footing wasn't possible. For added stability, one or two officers held onto the responders pulling the bodies out onto the tier.

Ziemer and the others worked quickly to get the victims out of Jackson's cell. Within minutes, I arrived on the scene, meeting up with Sellmer, Stewart and Luxford. We were armed and ready to take back the unit.

My state of shock at the horror I encountered when I walked into the Lockup had been interrupted by loud, profane threats from the inmates.

"You fucking pigs will die!" an inmate shouted in a voice heavy with hatred. Crouching behind the cloak of anonymity, these rioting cowards hid their identities as they crowded into cells toward the back of the south side.

"We got weapons and we ain't gonna stop!" they boasted.

At this point, we figured part of that was true. We had all heard the gunfire. But we had no idea how many weapons or how much ammunition the inmates had with them. We also knew they'd be armed with the other stabbing and slashing weapons that inmates typically use in these violent situations. Though the process may be slower and more excruciating, stabbing and slashing weapons are as deadly as a loaded gun. That we all knew full well.

The tier was a frenzied mess of confusion and frustration, as we had no direct view of the inmates. We ducked into the sergeant's office off the corridor to get our bearings. When my schedule changed several weeks prior, Saturdays became one of my regular days off. So I couldn't say for sure who was assigned to what post that day or who might have called in sick. I had no idea which officers were being tortured or killed at that moment. We later learned that three officers originally scheduled to be off that day were filling in for others in the Lockup.

We also had no idea how many inmates might be involved. We were firing questions at one another, hoping for answers that would give us a clearer picture. *Who's assigned to the AC today? Who are the escort officers today? Which inmates had been to the Visitor Center?*

I made a quick phone call to Dr. Phillip McNamara, the prison's chief medical officer. Though we'd later find his estimate was off, he said he had four dead officers in the hospital. But he didn't know who they were.

The situation was a sensory overload like none I'd ever experienced. Complete chaos wouldn't be an exaggerated description. But this is what we had all been trained for. It was fight or die trying. We took our positions at the front of the south side of the tier.

"We got pig hostages back here, you motherfuckers!" Each threat seemed louder and louder, like a Fourth of July fireworks show building to the big finish.

"Rubi!" we called out. We were only slightly sure Officer Rubiaco was in the building when the riot broke out. "Are you down there, Rubi?" we yelled out again. We heard all sorts of responses – but none from Rubi. We could only wonder if he somehow made it safely out of the unit, or we were simply too late.

The sound of officers responding to the scene surely thrust the inmates' fevered tempo into high gear. This type of criminal is not known for restraint and reason. Though noncompliant rioting inmates rarely adhere to rules, we attempted to talk them out.

"You know the policy on hostages! Turn 'em loose!" Lieutenant Sellmer shouted. By now, anger and urgency were running high on both sides of the grill gate.

Ignoring our direct orders, the inmates continued their revolution. While shouting back and forth, they hurled personal property out onto the tier. Though a cyclone of food, inmate property, and other debris littered the area, there was no significant destruction of the unit that we could see. No shattered windows, no fires smoldering. There just wasn't time for that. Killing or torturing officers was the first priority. And a taste for revenge fuels the brutal acts of rioting inmates like an adreneline shot to the arm.

Like writings on the wall, we all understood it now. The black revolutionary inmates had vowed revenge for the 1970 yard incident at Soledad that left three black inmates dead. The note found next to Officer Mills' battered body promising eye-for-an-eye retaliation and other similar threats were becoming a reality inside the Lockup. Inmates with a score to settle unleashed their vengeance on officers the moment Jackson had them freed from their cells.

◆

Meanwhile, the security concern wasn't limited to the Lockup unit.

There were more than three thousand general population inmates out on the yard getting ready to lock up for the afternoon count when Jackson started his revolution. The gunfire had them all cloistered in one corner, up against the fence, straining to see some action from the drama unfolding just beyond their reach.

Correctional Officer Steve Cambra was already scheduled to work that day but rushed in early to help out after hearing about the riot on the radio. He arrived about the time the general population inmates were coming back to the cell block from their daily assignments. Before Cambra entered the North Block, there were about five tiers of inmates standing around waiting to be celled up. That's about eight hundred inmates to one sergeant and two officers — all three unarmed.

Hearing the gunfire, most of the convicts ran to the northwest corner of the block, crowding around windows on the second, third, fourth, and fifth tiers. The block sergeant rang the emergency buzzer and called for an immediate lock up over the loudspeaker. Only a handful of inmates complied. He called the yard office for backup. Responding armed staff threw rifles up to the officers on the elevated gunrails to provide more coverage.

Outside, the injured and dead officers from the AC were being moved on gurneys to the hospital. Watching from inside, the voices of general population inmates rose into cheers like fans at a football game. "Kill all the pigs!" they shouted. Warning shots were fired from the officers on the gunrails to keep the situation from escalating into something worse.

Though the inmates cheered seeing the bloodied officers, once the bar was thrown and their cells opened, most walked right in to lock up. Inmates are quick to show verbal support of their rioting brothers. But when it comes down to jumping into the mix, most usually think twice. The inmates might not like the officers, but they sure as hell don't want convicts running the joint — especially the max-security inmates in the Lockup. Staff is the lesser of two evils.

Cambra and his fellow officers swiftly did their jobs and got the inmates locked up tight in their cells, restoring control to their area of the institution. Prison supervisors took the officers' keys after every last inmate was in a cell. Then they literally locked staff inside the building with the inmates, as was policy. You can't lose control of a prison if no one has the keys.

Elsewhere on the grounds, inmates in the open floor tiers of East Block acknowledged the riot by shouting, cheering, and throwing everything from their cells out onto the floor – books, clothing, papers, etc. They set fire to small clumps of paper to signal solidarity.

In the high-security B Section, inmates were flat-out refusing to lock up. Like other convicts on the property, they were emboldened by the atmosphere of chaos around the prison.

Arriving shortly before 3 p.m. for his regular shift, Sergeant Jim Butler was instructed to get a weapon from the armory and go straight to a gunrail in B Section. There he observed inmates on the second tier jamming the bar with their cell doors, preventing the lock up. Agitated, they shouted obscenities at the officers. Butler fired several warning rounds from his sub-machine gun into the roof to get the inmates to finally shut up and lock up.

Outside the prison, at the East Gate, responding units from the California Highway Patrol and the Marin County Sheriff's Department stood by at the ready and patrolled the perimeter roads. Offshore in the Bay, the Coast Guard was also on alert.

◆

"This will be over before sundown." Warden Heinze's stern advice from my early days in Corrections played over and over in my mind as I stood at the front of the tier in the Lockup. I knew we had to end this revolution before sundown or we'd surely have more casualties.

"We're going to kill you motherfuckin' pigs!" one of the inmates yelled out to us.

"Give it up, you son of a bitch!" An officer shouted back his own obscenities in a voice booming with anger so scorching you could almost feel the heat.

Again, they threw out their best threats. "We got weapons and we're gonna kill you bastards!"

"Well, then, you won't make it out alive!" I quickly responded, as calmly as if I had just solved a riddle. It sort of took me by surprise. At some point between the time I grabbed the weapon out of the armory and this very moment, I had exhaled to a feeling of complete calm. I was as composed as if I was out on a boat casting my line into the sea. I had no fear and was in complete control. It was an odd phenomenon, given the dire circumstances. For me, things strangely appeared to slow down to a manageable set of tasks. I knew what I had to do. And I knew nothing was going to harm me.

But I'd had more than enough of this inmate terrorism, enough of the stench of death inside that place. I wasn't about to let my tortured coworkers bleed to death in a cell at the end of the tier waiting for these maniacal convicts to surrender. Hoping to finally scare the rioting inmates the hell out of there, I repeated my promise to end their lives if they didn't immediately stop their killing spree.

"This is your last chance! Give up or we're coming down the tier for you!" Nothing. We could've heard ice cubes melting. Apparently, they needed more convincing.

Slowly, I dropped to one knee. I pulled my Thompson sub-machine gun up to my shoulder. Sellmer and Stewart stood strong as steel right behind me, their weapons engaged. With eyes on the target, they each shot one round from their rifles down the south side of the tier into the back wall. It was a move that would have frightened most sane people into surrender. But there's something foolishly defiant about hardened criminals on the rampage. Or maybe they figured they had nothing to lose. Still no response.

Aiming my weapon down the tier, I eyed my target with a steady arm. I had the delicate sense of the trigger. I could fire one or two or five rounds with steady control while the weapon was on full automatic. Most people don't have that reflex. For some reason, maybe just for this incident, God gave me that skill on the Thompson.

Carefully, I fired off a controlled burst of five rounds about a hundred feet straight down the middle of the tier and into a solid cell door that had been swung open. Though it only took about a second it seemed much longer. It felt like a slow-motion replay. *Kerthunk . . . kerthunk . . . kerthunk*. In real time, the sound is harsh and as loud as a firecracker, but the action seemed quiet and methodical as it played out in my head. And it made a definite impression in that cell door. The bullets tore through the 300 lb. steel door as though it was a cardboard cutout, leaving behind sharp jagged holes in their wake.

The Thompson also made an impression on the rioters. The sound of tearing metal scattered the inmates out of one cell and onto the tier like billiard balls on a strong, hard break. Finally, they got it. They knew we weren't playing games.

We held our fire as about twenty inmates ran for cover into another cell farther down the tier. They left the two severely injured hostages behind in the bloody chamber of horrors. The tier was still and quiet. The grunts and groans of assailants and victims had stopped.

Tortured and left for dead, Rubiaco and Breckenridge realized they were now alone in the cell. Their attackers had left the immediate area. The gunfire had been earth-shattering and promising at the same time.

But in that split second of the unknown, Rubiaco thought this was how and where he would die. For the first time since the attack began, he lifted his head to try and see Breckenridge. Rubi had been holding his head in a cocked position, trying to stop the bleeding around his slashed throat. Breckenridge was squirming out of the torn sheets that tied his hands together. His neck was marked by deep gashes and stab wounds. The strip of bedsheet the inmate used to try to strangle him was still hanging around his neck. Breckenridge immediately tried to untie the knot that held Rubiaco's feet to his handcuffed arms.

"That's too slow," Rubiaco half-whispered. "We'll both get it if we stay here any longer!" He looked around and noticed one of the inmate's razor-blade weapons lying on the bloodied floor. "Use that!" Rubi motioned toward the weapon. Breckenridge put the weapon to work, but the blade was dull and slow.

"Go faster!" Rubiaco begged him in a hushed but desperate tone.

"There's only one way to do it," Breckenridge told him. Grabbing the sheeting, he told Rubi, "Pull as hard as you can."

With what little strength he had left, Rubiaco pulled one way as Breckenridge pulled the other. Though it hurt like hell, Rubiaco kept from screaming out in pain. He knew if their attackers heard him, they might both be done for. Finally, the sheets tore apart from the handcuffs. The chance for survival was now or never.

"Let's go!" Breckenridge bolted first from the cell, followed closely by Rubiaco.

As the two ran down the tier, we instinctively yelled "Stop!" The shape these officers were in made them almost unrecognizable to us. Stripped of their uniforms and covered in blood, were these officers or inmates? Breckenridge had lost his eyeglasses in the attack, an accessory that always made him stand out.

Someone behind me yelled "Shoot them! Shoot them!"

"No! Hold your fire!" I yelled back without turning around. Suddenly, I recognized Rubiaco. If the other person running alongside him was an inmate, I thought, he wouldn't be able to overpower the three of us, armed and waiting.

Their faces were nearly ashen from the loss of blood. These were strong, young men, but they had just endured an assault most people would never survive. We weren't sure they'd make it to safety before passing out. If they didn't, we'd have to send officers down the tier to rescue them, putting more lives at risk. It wasn't an option we wanted to explore.

They moved as quickly as their battered bodies would allow toward me and the others at the front of the unit.

In the melee that followed Jackson's brief takeover, food carts had been tipped over by the rioting inmates, their contents strewn about the tier. In the scuffle of violence, garbage and blood had been smeared together on the floor. Footprints of the rioting inmates were etched in blood, as they moved from cell to cell on their charge.

Breckenridge made it safely to the front of the tier. But Rubi's feet slipped in the debris and he fell hard into an empty cell less than thirty feet from us. He was away from his captors now huddled in a cell at the end of the tier. But he was still far from safety.

Instinctively, I got up off my knee and made a move to help him. I couldn't see into it but I felt sure the cell was empty, except for Rubiaco. I had a weapon and could control the situation if there was an inmate in there. But somebody stopped me. One of the officers behind me grabbed the back of my shirt as I started down the tier. He likely thought I could lose the gun if confronted by an inmate hiding in that cell. It was a valid concern. I stayed put.

With his hands cuffed behind him, Rubiaco struggled to get up. His legs were wobbly, his constricted arms useless. The robust flow of adrenaline was the only source of strength his body could muster at that point. Finally, he made it out of the cell and to the front of the tier where familiar faces were waiting.

But Rubiaco was enraged.

"Those sons of bitches!" he screamed. The adrenaline that helped get him to safety was now propelling him to fight, fight, fight. His anger toward the inmates who had unleashed their violence on him and his coworkers was erupting like a volcano dormant for centuries. For Rubiaco, this behavior was uncharacteristic. But it was highly understandable considering what he'd been through.

"Give me a gun! I'll kill those bastards!" he shouted at us as he stood in the corridor, still bleeding and wobbly from the trauma. His body was trying to keep up with his mental state, which at this point was like a runaway train.

"No, Rubi! We'll take care of this," I assured him. "You get to the hospital."

Thankfully, he was still handcuffed. Though his hands were beginning to turn blue from the lack of blood circulation underneath the tight handcuffs, we rightfully decided to leave him that way until we could get him into the prison hospital.

Breckenridge had been helped out of the AC by a couple of officers. They made it as far as the yard office when he collapsed on the cement outside the door. He simply couldn't go any farther. He was still bleeding profusely and was now coughing up blood. Two officers arrived within seconds with another gurney and he, too, was rushed in to the hospital.

One officer pushing the gurney was his friend, Ted Zink. Lying on his side, Breckenridge knew he'd made it out of the war zone in the Lockup, but would he live through the nightmare? He lifted his head slightly and looked right into Zink's eyes.

"Ted . . . Pinell cut me."

Sergeant McCray was silent as medical staff applied pressure dressings to the lacerations on his neck and quickly wheeled him on a gurney to the prison hospital.

Inside the hospital, staff were bombarded with bodies and wounded officers like a military surgical unit suddenly under fire. Sergeant Bill McCuistion and staff quickly looked over the dead and injured as they came in, removing sets of prison keys if they were still attached to their uniforms, before rolling them into emergency rooms for treatment. Most of the wounds were undetectable at first glance, as they hid under copious amounts of blood, now drying on bare skin and clothing.

Sergeant Graham was wheeled into the hospital with his hands and feet still tied together. Medical staff noted "at least one large hole on the top of the head," and detected a faint pulse. They immediately began an external cardiac massage. Sadly, their efforts were unsuccessful. The veteran officer left behind a wife, four kids, and one grandchild.

Officers Krasenes and DeLeon, their hands and feet still bound, cords around their bloodied necks, were both dead on arrival at the prison hospital.

Breckenridge repeated, "Pinell stabbed me," to those tending to his wounds. With a punctured esophagus and fluid in his lungs, he was wheeled into surgery. Civilian and officer medical staff worked alongside an inmate surgery crew, starting IV solutions on Sergeant McCray and Officer Breckenridge, and applying sutures to the more obvious bleeders in their throat lacerations.

"Let me at those bastards!" Rubiaco continued his rantings inside the prison hospital, but his handcuffs were finally removed when he started to calm down. After initial care, Rubiaco, Breckenridge, and McCray were transported to Marin General Hospital for further treatment.

◆

After we got Rubiaco and Breckenridge out of danger inside the Lockup, I fired a second burst of ammunition down the south side of the tier into the back wall, just to let the inmates know we weren't going away.

None of us knew for sure if the attackers who were still crowded in a quiet cell at the far end of the tier were done with their attacks. They could come charging out at any moment brandishing weapons we still couldn't account for with any certainty. Was this part of their plan? Were they waiting for an ambush opportunity, knowing we'd charge onto the tier to try and save our fellow officers?

"All right, that's it!" I announced loudly. I'd run out of patience. The time had come to get these perpetrators out of the Lockup. We had to search each cell to fully account for remaining staff and inmates, as well as weapons and evidence. We couldn't do it until the rioters were moved out of there. But it had to be done carefully.

"Listen up!" I yelled down the tier. "Remove all your clothes and slowly walk out of the cell – one by one." I wasn't sure if they'd obey my direct order. Hatred and violence are hard to stop on a dime. They're even harder to reverse – especially when defeat is added to the mix. But we had a job to do and it didn't involve negotiating with a bunch of murderous inmates.

I stood there for a couple of seconds, waiting for a movement or sound from the other end of the building. A few more seconds passed. It felt more like several minutes before we saw the first face of an inmate peek out of the cell. He looked at us like a cat burglar caught in a patrol car spotlight. I couldn't see his hands at first so I braced myself and held my breath just as tightly as I held the Thompson. Naked, he slowly walked out. I yelled at him to put his hands in the air and turn around.

"Now walk backward up the tier toward us. And don't you dare slip or make any sudden moves," I warned. "If you do, I'll shoot you on the spot."

One by one, the inmates came down the tier backward. Their arms and hands, some with drying blood stains, rose above their heads and worked as rudders steering them around the remnants on the floor. Slowly and gingerly, they stepped in and around the debris. As they approached us, standing at the grill gate, they were told to turn around so we could get a front view of them to make sure they did not have any weapons on them of any sort hanging from their necks or tucked into their pubic hair. It's rare but it does happen.

When inmate Talamantez got to the front of the tier, I asked him if there were any more inmates down there hiding out. "Just one," he said with a glare of contempt. In the very likely chance he was lying, I yelled down the tier once more, "Come on out of there – NOW!" Sure enough, a few more inmates exited the cell, arms above their heads.

I figured Talamantez wouldn't be straight with us. I gave him a steely side-eye look that told him he wasn't getting away with anything. Responding officers cuffed him and the others before leading them out of the Lockup in a single line. One by one twenty inmates were marched over to the lawn in the plaza until they could be rehoused. There, several armed officers kept skillful watch over their every move.

Again, I yelled down the tier, ordering any remaining foolish inmates to exit the cell or face necessary force. There was no response. We felt it was then safe to give every last cell a closer look for any holdouts. Lieutenants Sellmer, Stewart, and I started slowly down the south side of the tier, our weapons pointing the way.

Ready for anything, we crept past cells 1-AC-51 . . . 52 . . . 53, stepping over garbage as we moved on. We strained to hear any signs of life coming from the cells ahead of us. I fired another burst of gunfire into an empty cell to alert any stubborn inmates that we were on our way down the tier and were formidably armed and fresh out of patience.

When the three of us got to cell 1-AC-63, we stopped. A glistening trail of blood painted the floor inside and outside the cell like a red carpet rolled out for the Devil himself. I peered inside and saw an officer's crumpled blood-soaked uniform on the floor. The shredded fragments of life in that cell were sickening – even to this experienced officer.

We slowly continued down the tier, safely up against the cell front. As we approached one of the last cells on the south side, I noticed a pair of feet in blue inmate stockings, barely poking out of the cell. Was he playing possum? I immediately ordered the inmate out. With no response, I jumped in front of the open door and fired three rounds into the back wall of the cell. Bam! . . . Bam! . . . Bam!

The white inmate, Ronald Kane, was already dead, sprawled across the bunk. His throat had been slashed so deeply that his head was almost severed from his torso. His blood still dripped from the lifeless body, soaking the mattress and pooling on the concrete floor. He and the other deceased white inmate, John Lynn, found outside Jackson's cell on the north side, were my tier tenders, also known as trusties. Though they were murderers and as cutthroat as the next guy, they were the lesser of many evils inside that building. For the most part, they were compliant prisoners. That earned them the job of tier tender. But trusties are typically perceived as *rats* by other inmates. It was likely that — and maybe the color of their skin — that got them killed.

August 21 turned out to be a cruel twist of fate for Kane and Lynn. They had been sentenced to life at San Quentin for a murder committed during an escape attempt. And they wound up being murdered during George Jackson's escape attempt.

After we had checked the last cell, we glanced into the rear stairwell next to the cell. Because the three of us were off duty that day, we didn't have the keys with us to go beyond the last cell and into the stairwell, where anyone could be hiding. We figured even if one of the rioting inmates got hold of an officer's set of keys, they wouldn't know which key was for the door to this stairwell. And they most likely wouldn't take the time to try them all. It appeared to be clear and secure, so we decided to move on to the other side of the tier.

As we walked back up the tier, I took a longer look inside each cell. I may never get those images out of my head. After all these years, if I close my eyes I can still see the bloodied uniform shirts and trousers on the floor, the harness trap for an officer's set of keys that had been ripped from a uniform, a co-worker's once pristine uniform hat desecrated as it lay in a pool of blood, and bloodied mattresses and other cell property thrown every which way. It looked as though a fiery hurricane from Hell had blown through that cell block.

Sellmer, Stewart, and I walked over to the north side, where we found two remaining inmates. They had barricaded themselves inside their cells when they heard the ruckus break out at the front of the Lockup. When Jackson ordered Officer Rubiaco to open all the cells, these two white inmates used torn bedsheets to tie their cell door bars closed so they wouldn't open with the others. They wanted no part of the rampage. They "locked" themselves in hoping to ensure their safety from the rioting inmates. It worked.

CHAPTER SIXTEEN

THE RIPPLE EFFECTS OF CHAOS

When the last of the inmates had been moved to the lawn, and the first floor of the Lockup had been secured as a crime scene, I was taking a breather in the sergeant's office. I removed my empty ammunition cartridges from my pocket.

After I had fired the short burst of machine gunfire into the steel cell door, I bent down and picked up my brass cartridges from the floor. This was an unconscious act. We were trained to retrieve any spent brass bullet casings whenever a weapon is fired inside the prison. We called it scooping the brass. This is to keep inmates from remanufacturing an empty cartridge into a live round of ammunition.

Strangely, as I picked up the Thompson's brass casings after the riot I unwittingly also picked up a 9-mm brass casing that was fired from the gun Jackson had used to kill Sergeant Jere Graham. And as I emptied my pocket, it tumbled out of its hiding place inside one of my 45-caliber casings. I gave the 9-mm brass casing to the deputy attorney general, where it joined other evidence as a piece of macabre history.

As I decompressed in the sergeant's office, another officer came up to me and offered to return the sub-machine gun – still securely in my arms – back to the armory.

"Noooooo," I said sternly, pulling it closer to my chest as if I were holding the cure for cancer. My reaction surprised me as much as it did the officer. That might have been the moment when the reality of it all set in. The adrenaline was not flowing as rapidly as it had been, and the level of danger had been lowered to a manageable everyday notch. I had time to breathe deeply and think about all that we had lived through that afternoon. Most of us, anyway.

I've read a lot over the years about extraordinary feats of courage, and they all speak to the rush of adrenaline that allows a person to charge in and do what needs to be done. In a riot situation, with lives at stake and time running out, courage must come from somewhere and quickly push fear aside. This was the most tragic and disastrous incident that I'd ever experienced in Corrections. Yet I had no fear as I ran into harm's way. None. Never in my life had I felt adrenaline at that magnitude. Not ever before or since that day. It was an odd sensation. I was calm and focused. Was that because I suspected an incident was coming for some time and my psyche had time to prepare? Maybe. But I knew exactly where I was going and what I was going to do when I got there. It was actually a comfortable feeling, not at all as anxious as you might think it would be.

A follow-up conversation with the prison psychologist assured me it was natural to feel that way during such an event. The adrenaline, he explained, is protecting you. It's the body's unique mechanism in dire situations. "But," he warned, "you don't want to subject yourself to that too often because it can kill you when your heart finally gives out." Good to know.

◆

Throughout the rest of the afternoon and into the evening, blood samples were taken from each of the inmates being held on the lawn in the plaza. In addition, any dried blood found on the inmates was carefully scraped off, secured, and tagged as part of the investigation. None of the inmates on the lawn was injured in the incident in the Lockup. The dried blood was that of the victims inside the AC.

In handcuffs and leg chains, the inmates were issued jumpsuits and given haircuts. No more hiding weapons in long or full heads of hair. From there, they were escorted one by one into the yard office for interrogation by prison officials. Typically, most declined to comment or said they knew nothing of Jackson's plan.

"I've got a headache," was inmate Pinell's only response when questioned about the incident.

By early evening, numerous outside law enforcement personnel had been dispatched to the prison to provide added security. Stationed all around the perimeter and on various roads leading away from the facility, they kept a tight vigil for suspicious activity and curious reporters and bystanders who got too close.

Inside, investigators from the state Department of Justice Criminal Identification and Investigative Services bureau, the Marin County Sheriff's Department, and the office of the Marin County district attorney collected fingerprints and other evidence as they combed through the wreckage that was the first floor of the Lockup.

Several officers were dispatched in shifts to Marin General Hospital to stand watch outside the rooms of Sergeant McCray and Officer Breckenridge. Officer Rubiaco received 110 stitches and was released. Being prepped for the lengthy stitching, he asked for a telephone. On what surely was the worst day of his life, Rubi phoned his girlfriend and proposed.

"When she said yes," Rubiaco told me later, "it suddenly became the best day of my life."

By 6 p.m., a white chalk outline of Jackson's body was all that was left in the roadway outside the chapel where his escape attempt was stopped.

By 7 p.m., the caravan of several hearses had left the prison hospital yard.

◆

A situation like the riot we experienced has a ripple effect on the entire institution. Uninvolved inmates on the second floor of the Lockup had to be relocated to another cell block to make room for the twenty-three inmates from the first floor. But before that, all personal property had to be removed from the cells on the second floor, boxed up, and placed in safekeeping.

Seventeen inmates from the second floor of the AC were temporarily moved to the South Block, about a hundred yards away. That housing section was also under my supervision. Unfortunately, we had to double-cell some of the inmates in Ad Seg – a move that was only allowed in emergencies. But it gave us the additional space we needed. Very carefully, we co-mingled the highest risk inmates in the facility, placing black inmates and white inmates together. Twenty-three convicts had to fit into seventeen cells. We paired a handful of them up as safely as we could under the circumstances, paying particular attention to their individual felon profiles. Then we hoped for the best. We didn't discriminate and we couldn't segregate. We just needed to get people locked up quickly. And we still had several thousand inmates to feed that evening.

Up on the second floor of the AC, the relocated inmates were chanting "Kill the pigs!" over and over, louder and louder – their bold attitude fueled by the fact that they were tucked safely inside their cells for the night. Cowards.

Harmless or not, I was in no mood for the distraction. I went up to the second floor, still holding on to the Thompson. As I walked down the tier and back up the tier, twenty-three pairs of eyes never left the weapon in my hands. Then I stopped and laid the barrel of the machine gun on the cross bar of a cell.

"Shut the fuck up," I ordered calmly but loudly.

We didn't hear another word from them the rest of the night. They didn't know it, but the Thompson was not loaded. I had removed the bullets before going up on the tier in the event I somehow lost possession of the weapon.

◆

The kids were asleep when I arrived home close to midnight. As I ran to the prison armory earlier that day, my mind was frantically trying to visualize what was happening inside the facility. When I walked into the Lockup, where my senses were instantly assaulted by the violence taking place, my priorities centered on rescuing hostages and securing the cell block. It wasn't until I walked through my front door in the now quiet night that thoughts of my wife and children flooded my tired mind.

Heading upstairs, I walked past our dining room where the paint cans, brushes, and drop cloths were right where I had left them earlier that afternoon. As I quietly dad-checked my children one by one, all sleeping peacefully in their beds, I marveled at my luck that I was coming home physically unharmed that night. Had the riot occurred a month earlier, before my days off had been changed, it would have been me in that cell block when Jackson started his deadly revolution. The thought didn't make me feel any better.

Instead, I felt deep sorrow for the wives and children of the decent, brave officers we had lost just hours earlier. These were fellows I worked with for months or years, officers I spoke with a day ago now gone in a gruesome manner at the hands of murderous criminals. I thought about how their families would never be the same – emotionally and financially. Many were one-income families in those days, and now their breadwinners were gone. In a matter of minutes three wives became widows and more than a dozen children were suddenly fatherless. I can't imagine how difficult it must have been to explain how the vicious actions of one person could set off a chain of violence that altered so many lives so quickly. And I couldn't help but wonder how

Shirley might explain it to our children if I had been one of the slain. I closed my eyes and shook my head to clear the unpleasant image from my mind.

Shirley was in bed, though not asleep, when I walked into our bedroom. Through the years, I've thought again and again about my quick comment to her after I got the phone call from the prison operator that afternoon: "Jackson's got a gun and he's loose in the prison!" Each time I replay it in my mind I imagine the fear she must have felt when she heard that, knowing I was about to rush into the middle of it.

Throughout the ordeal, Shirley and the kids kept watch, hoping all afternoon and into the evening to see Dad coming up the front steps. It wasn't until Shirley noticed the officers marching the naked inmates out of the building to the lawn that she enlisted our daughter Kim's help in ushering our two youngest girls and our son away from the big picture window upstairs. She must have known at that point that the insurrection was under control. But that could have only been slightly reassuring, as she still had no idea of my safety. It took a long time to restore order to the Adjustment Center and get all the displaced inmates back into cells. It was well after 8 p.m. before I could call her to let her know I was okay.

When I walked in she got up to embrace me. We both felt enormous relief, but we said nothing at first. So many thoughts were running at full speed through my head: the sixth sense I'd been grappling with for weeks, the switch in my days off that likely spared my life on this day, my injured and slain coworkers, the enormous tasks ahead of us to get the prison back to normal working order.

Finally, she turned to sit on the edge of the bed. I couldn't sit. I needed to move, to somehow walk off the toxic effects of the day. I was definitely exhausted, but I wasn't ready to sleep. The adrenaline was still pumping, and my brain was jam-packed with thoughts and observations on the long day.

I asked if she wouldn't mind taking some notes as I recounted for her the grim details of the riot, painting a grisly picture with ugly words and phrases that no longer startled her after so many years. Because I am such a history buff, I often kept notes about events or incidents, and Shirley was my notetaker as I talked through the experiences. She was a great one for keeping little diaries through the years, mostly about the silly things the kids did. But at times she put more serious words to paper. As I talked on and on about the incident, she wrote page after page.

Pacing back and forth in our bedroom, I relayed what I encountered when I ran into the Lockup: the sight of open empty cells, the inmates on the loose, the screams of hatred that bounced off the bloodied walls like growling echoes in a deep cavern. I told her of the shocking sight in the cells where the violence took place, the injured officers running for their lives up the tier, and my initial fear that my good friend Sergeant Ken McCray had been killed. Though they were critically wounded, I assured Shirley that Ken and Officers Rubiaco and Breckenridge had miraculously survived the vicious attacks. I stared at the floor as I described the torture they endured on that tier. Focusing on one small thread of carpet, I allowed the dark images of the day to flow out of my mind and soul in a sort of structured cleanse.

As Shirley and I talked for a couple of hours that Saturday night, I finally got to enjoy my chilled wine cooler that was supposed to be my reward for painting the dining room on my day off. It was a small bit of calm after a dreadful day that left many of us on edge for weeks.

CHAPTER SEVENTEEN

A PRISON RECOVERS

On Sunday morning I was right back at work in the Lockup, as San Quentin began the methodical process of recovery. I went about my duties alongside investigators taking photos of the tier and piecing together the fragments of the deadliest day California's Corrections profession had ever seen.

The investigation team had been hard at work since the moment the inmates were relocated out of the Lockup on Saturday. They tagged and processed bloodstained weapons, torn bedsheets, earphone cords, and other evidence in their meticulous search over every inch of that tier. Officers carefully gathered up the bloodied Corrections uniforms of injured coworkers and those who had made the ultimate sacrifice.

A select team of officers– the San Quentin Security Squad – conducted a detailed search of every cell on the first floor of the Adjustment Center. Even the toilets were thoroughly examined. During a search of the combo sink/toilet in cell 1-AC-8 on the north side of the tier, Officer Hal Bard felt a steel-wool-like substance hung up on the back side of the toilet's internal trap. Tugging at it, he pulled up the discarded wig that Jackson used to hide the gun on top of his head. It was Hugo Pinell's cell.

All inmate property was carefully removed from the twenty-six occupied cells. The materials were itemized, boxed, and stored in a room on the third floor of the AC. The lock on that room was changed, and the one new key was secured by a correctional lieutenant.

◆

Several of my fellow officers and I had planned to attend the funerals of the three officers killed in Jackson's uprising – even though two of the services were scheduled for the same day. We didn't want to miss an opportunity to show our respect for their supreme sacrifice in the line of duty.

The first memorial service was for Frank DeLeon on Tuesday, August 24. The second was for Paul Krasenes in Novato on Thursday, followed by Jere Graham's service in Sonora later that afternoon. In solidarity, we lined up shoulder to shoulder. Standing tall, we were proud though still grieving. We saluted our fallen comrades as the pall bearers carried the caskets slowly past us, knowing full well it could have been any one of us instead. There were approximately 250 mourners in attendance at each service, including about 100 uniformed correctional staff.

During the Krasenes memorial, Associate Warden James Park walked down the line in back of us and quietly told us to return to the prison as soon as the service was over. Protesters had been gathering outside the East Gate of San Quentin. A crowd control squad was needed on the grounds to keep things from getting out of hand. I had planned to drive to Sonora immediately following the Krasenes funeral to attend Sergeant Graham's memorial. But because of the growing swarm of demonstrators, we all had to return to the institution to provide added security.

"The bastards won't even let us bury our dead officers peacefully!" I shook my head as we piled into our cars and headed for the highway.

When we arrived back at the prison, we were met by nearly three hundred demonstrators outside the East Gate protesting the death of inmate George Jackson. Largely comprised of white individuals, with a few celebrity faces such as activist Tom Hayden and actress Jane Fonda thrown into the mix, it was mostly just a bunch of rag-tag radicals trying to incite anarchy. Dutifully, we formed a line of defense just inside the East Gate.

We had a well-trained, well-organized control squad of fifteen officers who worked as a team to prevent any incursion that might flare up. I was the point man on the squad. In addition, we were backed up by the local sheriff's office, as well as some additional armed correctional officers just out of sight in a vacant house on prison grounds. In the unlikely event the protesters got past our line of defense, the armed officers would be there to stop the invasion from escalating into something much worse. But our squad was well prepared to stop them where they stood at the East Gate.

And what a nasty, foul-mouthed bunch of thugs they were! They glared at us, nostrils flaring, insults and spittle flying out of angry mouths. Again, we stood in defense of our facility and the surrounding community as these protesters called us filthy pigs and hurled their vile threats at us. In typical bullying fashion, one particular loudmouth kept up a string of dastardly promises to ram right over us and storm the gate.

Eventually, I'd had all I was going to take. I took two steps forward from the crowd control line to get closer to this jerk. I narrowed my eyes, aiming my focus past his pupils and into his soul.

"Ok, if you're that anxious to meet your maker today, go ahead and cross this line," I told him, growing taller on a deep breath. I could almost hear the wheels turning inside his brain. He gave a second thought to his boasting, quieted down, and never did try to charge the line of officers. I'm sure that was the smartest decision he'd made all day.

A week after the riot, as protests continued outside the prison walls, a handful of outsiders were finally allowed to come into the institution and meet with officials. The outsiders included a medical professional and community and state government leaders. They met with Corrections Director Ray Procunier and toured the Lockup. Following the tour, they each spoke with the press and addressed the demonstrators.

It's been my experience that outsiders are seldom helpful at a time like this. But one visitor in this group surprised me: then-California Assemblyman Willie Brown.

As a black youth growing up in the small, segregated town of Mineola, Texas, Brown more than survived the racial unrest in his community – he thrived. A graduate of San Francisco State University, he went on to get his law degree at Hastings College. During the late 1950s, Brown, by then a Democrat, opened a law firm in San Francisco. There, he practiced criminal defense law and became involved in the Civil Rights movement that was rolling across the nation.

Brown has been a well-known political activist throughout California for decades. He began a long and storied political career in the California State Assembly in 1964, eventually becoming Speaker of the Assembly, a title he would hold for nearly fifteen years. Before his retirement from politics, Brown served two terms as mayor of San Francisco from 1996 to 2004. He is widely recognized and well liked in left-leaning Marin County.

The fact that Brown was a black Democrat, coupled with the racial undertones surrounding the protest, some of us holding back the angry crowd didn't have high hopes when he stepped out on the Post Office steps to speak to the protesters. To his credit, instead of creating more drama, he assured them he was confident the tragic incident was handled with the utmost professionalism. He explained the armed prison staff were simply doing their jobs and there didn't appear to be any issues of concern for them to protest.

Given his history, Brown could have really stirred the pot that day, but he didn't. Instead, he diffused the situation in a composed, nonpartisan manner. Following his remarks, the protest slowly fizzled out.

As the group dispersed and we relaxed our position of crowd control, an FBI agent I had been talking with revealed that one in three demonstrators there that day was actually an informant with the FBI. Their assignment was to blend into the group and lend support if necessary. Turns out, I needn't have worried so much. The crowd came equipped with its own built-in security system.

◆

The institution-wide lockdown of all inmates that was ordered immediately after the riot remained in effect for a week. All days off for officers were cancelled until further notice. Shifts were recalculated to overlap one another by a couple of hours. Inmates were cell-fed all meals for several days, and the institution was closed to all visitors until the following Saturday. There was no inmate movement whatsoever. Throughout the week, outside law enforcement agencies continued to provide additional security to the perimeter of the prison.

Days later, inmate workers would meticulously scrub the dried blood stains of a cell block murder scene, where over the course of mere minutes five victims spoke their last words.

But even before the blood had dried investigators began individual recorded staff interviews of the incident. All officers and other staff members on the prison property when the riot broke out were interviewed at length – regardless of where or what shift they had worked. Beginning the evening of the riot, nearly 125 people answered investigators' questions, describing everything they saw and heard.

Officer Rubiaco was interviewed at home late in the evening on August 21. Investigators conducted a ninety-minute interview with Rubiaco as he recuperated from his wounds. Sergeant McCray's interview was conducted bedside in his hospital room two days after the riot. Because of his extensive throat wounds,

Breckenridge wasn't interviewed until ten days after the riot while he was still hospitalized.

I sat down with departmental investigative Lieutenants Paul Dobreff and George Watkins on Sunday, the day after the riot. They listened intently and recorded my thoughts as I told them about my every move on Saturday, what I witnessed, and what role I played in bringing the riot to an end.

"I made the decision on my own to go get the Thompson sub-machine gun and do whatever it takes to stop Jackson," I told the lieutenants at one point in the interview. "And I didn't stop to ask anyone's permission."

Dobreff motioned toward Watkins to turn off the tape recorder.

"Are you sure of that statement, Lieutenant?" Dobreff asked me.

"Damn sure," I answered.

"Well, I hope you don't lose your job over this," he cautioned.

"I don't give a shit. I did what had to be done."

When an inmate is armed and on the loose there's no time to ask permission. If you have some authority and you don't abuse it just a bit at the right time for the right reasons, you're probably not leadership material. I may have put a few holes in the wall and damaged a state-owned cell door in the process, but I didn't add to the loss of life.

Above all else, I knew that riot had to be stopped before the sun went down.

◆

Not long after the riot, while the prison and staff were still recovering, we were all trying to put the incident behind us and get the facility back to business as usual. I was working my regular assignment, going about my duties back and forth between the north side and the south side of the complex.

I noticed that each time I stepped out of the Lockup, a couple of Hells Angels inmates were standing nearby. They walked along with me, one on either side of me, as we talked briefly about the weather and what not, all the way across the yard to the South Block. When I left that building to return to the Lockup, there they were again. And again, we walked together across the yard back to the Adjustment Center. This went on for several weeks.

At first it seemed odd: the same Hells Angels right there in the same spot every day. But it didn't take me long to figure out what they were doing.

After the August 21 riot, some of the Black Panther inmates had put out a contract to have me killed in protest over the death of their quasi-leader, George Jackson. Though I wasn't one of the officers who shot Jackson to stop his escape attempt, I was in charge of the Lockup and took part in ending the riot and the killing spree. So I was the enemy, more now than ever before.

As is typical in prison, word of that threat traveled quickly around the facility. Almost immediately, it caught the attention of the Hells Angels inmates who never forgot the day in early 1970 when I listened to their request and orchestrated the release of their friend Al Passaro back into general population. They weren't about to let any assailant get within three feet of me as I moved around the facility.

The Angels were a loyal bunch.

CHAPTER EIGHTEEN

HISTORY'S HARSH LESSONS

I've been asked many times over the years why I didn't kill the rioting inmates when I charged in there that day with a Thompson sub-machine gun. After all, people have argued, these violent criminals had killed three of my coworkers, and they might have killed or tortured more if not stopped with lethal force. My only response to that is simple: That wasn't my intent. Unlike the rioters, my urgency was not fueled by revenge.

There was a higher purpose to my mission and it didn't involve killing inmates to stop a riot. I had a job to do and I knew I could get it done *without* further bloodshed. Rescue the hostages and restore order in the cell block – those were tasks one and two of my job duties in that dire situation. My decisions were based on more than a decade of experience and complete confidence in my skills as a Corrections professional.

I was neither reprimanded nor commended by my superiors for my actions on August 21. None of us were. Warden Nelson was traveling up north when he received news of Jackson's escape attempt and the subsequent riot. Though he cut short his vacation and returned to the institution immediately, he and I didn't discuss the incident until the next day, when we went over the riot and the casualties in great length. The warden neither praised nor criticized my actions, nor did he try to Monday-morning quarterback what I did with the machine gun that day in the

Lockup. Though he never came right out and said it, I had the distinct feeling he was supportive of my actions. And that was enough for me.

Naturally, I've had second thoughts in the years following the riot about what could have been done prior to the incident that might have made a difference in the outcome that day. But without the benefit of hindsight, we're left to rely on sixth sense alone. Still, the questions kept swirling around in my head.

Could we have somehow prevented the riot in the first place? Or was George Jackson so focused on a revolution that no amount of prevention was going to stop him? What if Officer Rubi Rubiaco and Sergeant Ken McCray hadn't been so observant, noticing the shiny glint of something poking out of Jackson's hair?

Because I was in charge of the Lockup, could I have been more vigilant with my officers to make sure cells were searched more often? I had enough floor staff who could go through two or three cells per day; should we have conducted more searches?

The amount of property that can accumulate in a convict's cell is staggering. From magazines, newspapers, and assorted books, to plastic utensils, writing supplies, clothes, and mountains of snacks and toiletries from the canteen. Some of these guys could have opened their own corner dime stores!

Jackson surely had far too much property in his cell, including bundles and bundles of newspapers and magazines that he tied together to use as weightlifting equipment. And though some were in prison storage, he had over a hundred books. Many were stacked high like miniature skyscrapers in a cement and steel landscape.

After August 21, investigators found a 22-caliber gun barrel secreted inside a large block of cheese tucked away in Jackson's cell. Ammunition for the gun he used in his deadly escape attempt was found secreted inside bars of soap sitting innocently on a shelf in his cell. He had poked holes into the soap and pushed live ammunition into them so they wouldn't be found in a routine cell search. How that gun barrel and ammunition were introduced into the prison and landed in Jackson's hands is anyone's guess.

And he wasn't the only one who squirreled away dangerous contraband. Numerous objects found in the other cells on the first floor of the Lockup revealed various criminal plots in the making: a set of officer's keys tucked between the blanket and the mattress, a set of officer's keys rolled up inside a towel, one razor blade under the mattress and another shoved inside the flap of a cardboard box, three doctored pen cartridges, a note depicting the layout of the fourth floor of the hospital – including the condition of each inmate residing there, and an escape route map secreted inside a package of pipe cleaners.

Jackson was obviously trying to make it back to the privacy of his cell with the gun undetected when his plan was foiled by the keen eyes of officers in the Lockup. When the investigatory cell search revealed the bars of soap hiding the bullets, we knew he had other plans for the weapon.

New questions cropped up. What was Jackson's Plan A? Would it have been successful? Would it have been deadlier than the Plan B he unleashed in the Lockup? And would it have involved innocent citizens outside the prison walls, perhaps in a San Francisco courtroom?

I never considered Jackson a celebrity of sorts, as others did – inside and outside the walls of San Quentin. He was just another prisoner in my max-security cell block. Though his revolutionary tendencies were alarming, they were not unique. The rising racial tension not just in San Quentin but around the nation was tangible. It was reason enough for a heightened observation of Jackson's comments, visitors, and alliances with revolutionary extremists of the time – even without the numerous red flags waving wildly right under our noses.

But I believe we all underestimated Jackson's treachery.

◆

In 1971, Associate Warden Park was under pressure from inmate lawyers and other visitors with regard to visitation and inmate rights in general at San Quentin. The lawyers' constant demands for changes to the visitation process – changes I and many other officers saw as nothing but a push to remove major security procedures – chipped away at Park's administrative layer until they reached his softer, more liberal underbelly.

For whatever reasons – and we'll never know them now – Park and others repeatedly relaxed the policies for George Jackson and some of his revolutionary comrades – not a good road to take with the likes of those convicts. If Jackson's visitors were denied a visit for various valid reasons, they simply crossed the street to Park's office and lodged a complaint. Without a nod to policy, and often without any discussion with the officers involved, Park agreed to the demands of the visitors.

Retired Folsom Prison Warden Glenn Mueller warns against that kind of action. "When the convicts can figure out ways for you to violate your own procedures, that's when you'll get beat," he told me. "They don't choose the strongest link to go up against, they choose the weakest," he added. "You never, ever reduce your max-security procedures."

The 2015 incident at the max-security Clinton Correctional Facility in Dannemora, New York, where two inmates escaped with the help of willing staff members who violated prison procedures, is strong evidence of that.

In the aftermath of the riot, I spoke at length with the state deputy attorney general and staff from the Marin County district attorney's office. But when Corrections officials rushed to the facility after being notified of the riot, most didn't think it necessary to talk directly to me about the incident.

As a key figure in the restoration of order in the Lockup after an extraordinary incident, you'd think someone would want to hear my thoughts, person-to-person. Even Associate Warden Park, whom I hadn't spoken with since we both heard the gunfire while standing on our front lawns, never asked what I knew, what I saw, what I did. And state Corrections Director Ray Procunier never approached me about the major prison riot that rocked a state agency under his supervision.

I adamantly believe communication is key in the prison business – on all levels. Communication between staff and administrators, as well as communication between officers and inmates, are both critical to maintaining a smooth operation.

But even as the blood was drying on the cell block walls of the Lockup, and responders and other staff were conducting business with the highest professionalism under the cruelest circumstances, the administration still didn't get that one simple principle. For the rest of my career I wondered if they ever would.

Thankfully, after August 1971, officers and administrators started to pay more attention to red flags – at San Quentin, at least. And they gave more credence to the role sixth sense plays in correctional settings. But as my generation was heading into retirement, the newer prison designs chipped away at the opportunities for communication between convicts and staff. When you take away the exercise in understanding the element, you're going to have problems. Officers need to see the inmates, to talk to them, to know what's going on. The reliance on gut instinct – one of the greatest tools in the business – was beginning to weaken like a Bay Area fog bank in the afternoon sun.

If the early observations and concerns of San Quentin staff had held more credence to prison officials, especially in the weeks leading up to August 21, that day likely would have ended differently. There's a very good possibility Jackson wouldn't have gotten his hands on a weapon.

But they didn't. And he did.

Today, around the country, cities are experiencing the alarming results of widening gaps between wealth and poverty, discord among races, and the subsequent dangerous division between law enforcement and the public.

As cultural and societal differences of a more modern era seem to be dividing our neighborhoods once again, we are left to wonder if it could lead to a resurgence of the violence we saw in my era. Will America's correctional facilities – and the people living and working inside them – fall victim to a catastrophic event that could finally spill over prison walls into our communities? How safe are we? How far have we really come from 1971?

To those who think today's institutions are safer and too sophisticated to fall to the cultural violence we saw in the 1960s and '70s, all I can say is I hope you're right. But if it's true that history repeats itself because we didn't listen the first time around, then sooner or later history will teach us.

Would more frequent cell searches, stricter safety measures, and increased communication have been enough to save the lives we lost in August 1971? That may be just one of a handful of questions that will forever haunt those of us who survived that terrible day.

◆

In early September 1971, California's Corrections community was still healing from the fresh wound of August 21. But three thousand miles away, officers at Attica Correctional Facility were about to experience one of the worst tragedies in American law enforcement history.

On September 9 – not three weeks after San Quentin's riot in the Lockup – nearly 1,300 New York inmates rioted over better living conditions and many other demands, taking control of the maximum security facility built in 1930. The shocking story of the Attica prison riot has been the subject of hundreds, if not thousands of books, films, documentaries, and print and online news articles and essays over the years. Some of those depictions do the complex story justice; others do just the opposite.

To adequately tell the full story here would take a massive volume of pages. What is important to note, however, is Attica's most glaring detail – it was a textbook example of what *not to do* when a prison riot breaks out. From the officials' complete failure to end the riot before sundown on the first day, and acknowledging hostages and bringing in outsiders to negotiate with hostage takers, to the jaw-dropping method in which they finally reclaimed control of the facility on the fifth day, Attica was an outrage on many levels. And in between, the incident was a true crime story rife with cultural, racial, political, and administrative conspiracy.

"The riot at San Quentin happened at the worst possible time," observed retired Corrections expert Steve Cambra, who was working as an officer in North Block that day. "When that riot broke out, all working inmates were returning from their assignments and everyone was moving about the cell block. The scene at Attica was similar. The inmates were all coming back from chow," he explained.

"But Attica didn't have the same gun coverage as California," Cambra added, noting the New York prison didn't have interior gun coverage in the living units to force lockup. California has gun coverage anywhere inmates can congregate in large groups, including living units, dining halls, and yards.

"California is often taken to task for their gun policy," Cambra stated, "but the reality is when the shit comes down it's good to have it. August 21 is proof of that."

Don Almeter was a new officer at Attica, only about sixteen months into the job, when the riot broke out on September 9. He was taken hostage by the inmates, stripped naked, blindfolded, and beaten with iron pipes and two-by-fours. The memory is as vivid today as it was forty-five years ago.

"We knew we were in trouble when that first day passed and nobody came for us," recalled Almeter, who was held in the "hostage circle" with about forty others, including officers and civilians. "The longer time went on, I knew that when they do finally come it's not going to be pleasant."

When state officials finally ordered an army of law enforcement to use lethal force on September 13 to storm Attica and regain control, thirty-nine people died in the deluge – including ten correctional staff being held hostage by inmates. Another officer and three inmates had been killed by inmates when the riot erupted. It was clearly a history lesson of the harshest kind.

"The year 1971 represents a watershed period in Corrections, as it was the height of a national revolutionary and anti-authority movement that spilled over into our jails and prisons," esteemed Corrections expert Carl Larson stated in 2013. "In that time, nearly two dozen staff were murdered in the American correctional system. It was a dark and bloody time in our nation's history, a challenging and agonizing year for those who worked the toughest beat in law enforcement. The riots at San Quentin and Attica reflect on how precious life is in deadly correctional uprisings."

Larson spent more than a half-century in Corrections, beginning as an officer at San Quentin, eventually working his way up to warden and director of the Planning and Design Division. And in that time he became an expert in hostage situations. He created a set of nine principles for managing correctional hostage incidents. Chief among those critical points is DO NOT acknowledge hostages. Prisons must have a strict no-hostage policy. It doesn't necessarily mean inmates will never take another hostage during an incident. But it lets the inmates know in no uncertain terms there will be no negotiating over hostages. That alone makes it much easier to end a riot before sundown.

California has a firm no-hostage policy. If New York had a similar policy in 1971, they didn't enforce it on September 9. As a result, the Attica riot ran four days longer than it should have to its devastating end.

EPILOGUE

A DEPARTMENT EVOLVES

"If history were taught in the form of stories,
it would never be forgotten."
—Rudyard Kipling

When the Department's investigation and interviews of the San Quentin riot were finally complete, the resulting official incident report ran more than five hundred pages – single spaced. It is an unprecedented piece of our history, as it indelibly marks the day that forever changed a profession.

The Marin County district attorney's office ended up charging six inmates with murder, conspiracy, and assault for their involvement in the August 21 riot. The San Quentin Six, as they would become widely known, included Hugo Pinell, Johnny Spain, Luis Talamantez, Willie Tate, David Johnson, and Fleeta Drumgo.

I was in charge of the inmate escort detail for the pretrial phase. The shackled defendants were transported in a panel truck, chained inside for their safety and to discourage assaultive behavior. Armed officers led in one vehicle and brought up the rear in another, sandwiching the heavily guarded truck as it made its way through crowded city streets bustling with typical workday traffic. We used two-way radios to converse with one another as we made our way from the prison to the jail and courthouse in the Marin County Civic Center.

The lead car and the tail car parked outside the sally port entrance to the jail. We signaled the jail officer, who opened the gate for us. Our armed officers escorted the inmates two at a time out of the truck and into the elevator for the ride up to the courthouse. I stood at the ready with my shotgun.

Inmate Hugo Pinell got out of the truck. Like the other inmates, he was in leg irons and a waist chain that looped around his neck and down his back. His arms were handcuffed to his waist chain. We weren't taking any chances.

"I could take that away from you," Pinell sneered, suddenly lunging toward me and the weapon in another of his attempts to strike fear. In all of that restraint gear, with not the slightest chance of victory, he still drew the only sword he had — intimidation.

With my finger firmly and visibly on the trigger of the shotgun, I held it up to him, placing the nose of the weapon directly under his chin.

"Don't do that," I said calmly. "Don't do that."

The sixteen-month trial, which cost more than $2 million, was the longest trial in California history at the time. The actual trial didn't begin until 1974, as a Marin County grand jury and the state appeals court first weighed in on discrimination claims.

When it ended in 1976, only inmate Johnny Spain, who had run out of the Lockup with George Jackson, was convicted of murder. Although he didn't shoot, strangle, stab, or slash any of the dead inmates and officers in the Lockup, he was convicted of conspiring with Jackson in the escape attempt that caused the deaths.

Of the other five inmates indicted in the case, two were convicted of assault on correctional officers, and three were acquitted of all charges.

Jackson's attorney, Stephen Bingham, who was Jackson's visitor earlier in the day on August 21, became a prime suspect as authorities tried to determine how Jackson got hold of a weapon. However, when the first news of the riot broke on radio and television airwaves, Bingham immediately fled the country and remained in hiding for thirteen years. He returned in 1984 to stand trial on charges of smuggling a weapon into a prison. He was ultimately acquitted in 1986.

◆

I realized George Jackson's failed attempt at a revolution wouldn't mean the end of assaults, riots, or other incidents that are just an accepted part of working in Corrections. After all, there is no real good feeling about this line of work. It's a negative environment. There's no getting around that.

But I knew I would no longer have to listen to Jackson's snide remarks about a rising dragon and a grand revolution that were nothing more than hate-fueled threats of violence and revenge. The riot was the end of the significance of the revolutionary movement of prison gangs in California, especially the Black Panthers. Today, prison gangs such as the Black Guerrilla Family, Mexican Mafia, and the Aryan Brotherhood remain a force to be reckoned with, but the grand plan of a takeover of the prison system ended that day in a thunderous defeat. It was a shock to the most incorrigible inmate conscience.

About fifty years ago, a Corrections official asked San Quentin's Warden Louis Nelson how many changes he'd seen in the profession during his long career, to which he boldly replied, "Too many to mention, and I can't recall one that I ever approved of."

Almost immediately after the riot, then-California Governor Ronald Reagan sent a handful of officials to San Quentin to discuss how to prevent another deadly uprising. We talked at great length about the staffing, security, and training it takes to work in the Department's maximum security units.

Fortunately, they took my suggestions to heart. And on September 8, 1971, oddly one day before the Attica riot erupted, Governor Reagan issued a proclamation in response to the deadly riot in San Quentin's Lockup.

Executive Order No. R-33-71 declared California's correctional facilities were housing a greater percentage of violent offenders than ever before, and "these forces constitute a real and present threat to an orderly correctional system."

More important, the decree stated the violent offenders pose "a significant threat to the life and safety of correctional personnel far beyond the potential danger to which such personnel have always been subjected in the past."

The proclamation promised a definitive review by the Board of Corrections of the August 21 escape attempt at San Quentin, as well as other violent incidents at San Quentin, Soledad Prison, Folsom Prison, and other institutions over the prior two years. The goal: to make recommendations regarding officer safety, unnecessary exposure of officers to danger, inmate security, inmate handling procedures, and communications with prisoners – including visits – all in the name of halting the violence within the state's prisons.

The Reagan proclamation was an unprecedented move, and one that gave us hope for the necessary changes to the Department's policies and procedures many of us knew were long overdue. The changes that came about within Corrections following the 1971 riot at San Quentin were significant in that California's policymakers finally recognized the magnitude of the inherent element of danger within the profession. The administration promised more safety measures for officers and others who work behind the wall. Thanks to the Reagan proclamation, prison staffing and money for training both saw increases – two critical areas where safety is concerned.

Specifically, the new safety measures at San Quentin included:

- All officers were issued a set of handcuffs. Prior to August 21, 1971, most officers didn't carry them as a general rule.
- After the riot, every inmate housed in the Adjustment Center was handcuffed when escorted anywhere (this was a statewide change).
- Staffing in the Security Housing Unit (SHU) was greatly enhanced.
- The Security Squad increased to eleven members.
- Transportation details were beefed up. All off-reservation transportation details went from one armed officer to two.
- The Correctional Officer Academy orientation was established for new cadets: a six-month probation period rotating all three watches (shifts).
- Visiting room procedures were enhanced; unclothed body searches were mandated for all inmates, not just max-security inmates.
- The Visitor Center was remodeled so that all max-security inmates received visitors in a no-contact-visit situation with bullet-proof glass between the inmate and visitor and a telephone for communicating back and forth. This included any visits with legal representatives.
- In addition, a sally port entrance was installed at the front door of the Adjustment Center, and the barred cell fronts in the AC were all replaced with solid steel cell fronts to limit contact with max-security prisoners.

Changes implemented within all correctional facilities statewide included:

- Mandatory training for officers on the Thompson sub-machine gun.

- More than two hundred staff were added to cover maximum security positions.

- The Department expanded the Joint Task Force on the intelligence network within the Corrections system to better identify and manage the inmates with gang affiliations. In addition, each facility had its own investigation team or unit. The Task Force expansion was the birth of the Department's documentation and certification process of gang members in California prisons.

◆

There are some correctional officers who seldom entertain the thought that a deadly incident like San Quentin's riot could happen to them. And there are others who think about it every time they walk through the gate.

Almost immediately following the riot in the Lockup, approximately twenty correctional staff quit their jobs with the Department of Corrections. Many were too traumatized by the incident to want to stick with prison work. In those days, the Department gave you five days to reconsider a decision to resign. Of those nearly twenty who left, only one came back.

On the night of the riot, B.J. Kennedy finally got a minute to run outside to the pay phone and call his wife.

"I told her there had been a significant riot, but that I was OK," the now-retired sergeant told me. She was relieved but asked him to quit his job that night, just resign and walk out.

"No way!" Kennedy exclaimed to his wife. "Someone has to stay. And right now it's the safest joint in the state!"

In October 1971, an opening came up on the Security Squad at San Quentin. I immediately asked for the job move. I needed something different after the August riot. For my mental well-being, as a way to decompress, I needed a change of scenery. The Security Squad had free run of the institution with no specific hours. We worked where needed: prisoner transport, search, etc. Like the first fall chill off the Bay, the job change was a welcome breath of fresh air.

◆

I've always believed the work of the uniformed peace officer is an honorable duty. I felt that way as a young man in 1959 when I first put on a Corrections uniform and I still feel that way today. Corrections is as important to public safety as any other uniformed law enforcement faction in our country.

Corrections may be just one cog in the wheel of administration of law and order but it is nonetheless a vital element in our vast criminal justice system. It must be recognized as such by the public, by the media, and by our partners in public safety if we're going to be successful in keeping our communities safe. Without correctional officers, who's minding the store? Who will step up to keep convicted criminals away from the law-abiding public?

Because he was just three years old at the time, my son, Jeff, doesn't remember that fateful Saturday in August 1971. He does, however, recall me describing the event over the years to interested family and friends, and at the occasional speaking engagement or documentary interview. And darned if he didn't follow in his old man's footsteps, carving out a career of his own in Corrections.

On one of his first assignments as a new officer, Jeff found himself in the Adjustment Center at San Quentin. He slipped his fingers into the machine gun bullet holes in the cell door that I had shot up that abysmal afternoon in 1971. He rubbed his hand across the bullet holes, their jagged steel edges now colored in rust. He couldn't help but visualize the intensity as his father and other responders regained control of a chaotic cell block and saved a prison.

Later, I told him I wished I could've taken that door home with me as a keepsake of that day. Much to my surprise, Jeff wrote to then-state Corrections Director Cal Terhune and asked if there was any way to make that happen.

"Give Dick Nelson anything he wants," the director told his staff.

Though the memories of my forty years in Corrections are sporadically interrupted with flashes of tragedy and loss, all in all it was a good job, a good career – just as I had been told it would be.

Shirley and I never fought about politics or religion or money – not once in our marriage. The day I finally retired in 1998, my long-devoted wife handed me our checkbook and a stack of bills like she was bestowing an award.

"Here . . . now it's your job," she declared. I willingly took over the task. I knew better than to argue.

Shirley was diagnosed with terminal thyroid cancer in March 2014. Our children rushed to her side and were an enormous help to us both. Every one of them took a leave of absence from work to spend precious time with her and help provide 24-hour care. They took turns sleeping in a recliner next to her bed so they could be close by whenever she needed attention.

One day in late September, true to her spirit, she mustered the strength to go into the kitchen and do what she loved: cooking for her family. She had a genuine passion for feeding others, and the years she spent in front of a stovetop had made her a four-star chef, at least in our eyes. Twenty-four hours later she was gone.

Shirley was the consummate wife and mother. And she was the love of my life.

Though long retired now, I'm never far from the profession and the brave men and women who choose it. And those who gave their lives in service to it are often in my thoughts. I walked away without a scratch from an historic insurrection that destroyed dreams, devastated families, and woke the sleeping giant of indifference in Corrections. I count myself one of the lucky ones.

As I look around my surroundings, I heave a sigh of relief and gratitude. I spent four decades in an important, dangerous job that provided a good living for my family and filled me with pride. Who could ask for more?

I also notice my dining room needs painting. But I think I'll go fishing instead.

END

A couple of my San Quentin coworkers in the Adjustment Center: Officer Urbano 'Rubi' Rubiaco and Officer Chad Breckenridge. Both were taken hostage and tortured by rioting max-security prisoners on August 21, 1971.

After the riot, the first floor of the Adjustment Center was littered with meal trays, debris, and blood-soaked clothing.

A long trail of blood painted the floor outside the cells on the North Side of the Lockup after the August 21, 1971, riot.

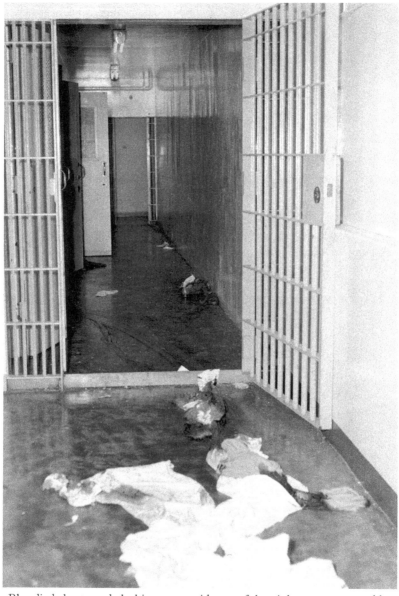

Bloodied sheets and clothing were evidence of the violence perpetrated by more than twenty max-security prisoners after armed inmate George Jackson ordered officers to release them from their cells.

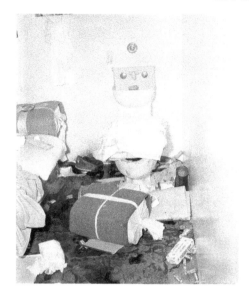

The images of carnage inside and outside George Jackson's cell in the Lockup
define the tragic story of revenge, torture, and death.

Once the riot had been stopped and the Lockup was back under the control of officers, the rioting max-security inmates were marched out of the AC and held on the lawn outside the building. Only then could the meticulous work of investigating a cell block crime scene begin.

Three rusted bullet holes in a cell door serve as a stark reminder of
the 1971 incident that left a prison reeling and brought needed changes
to the profession statewide.

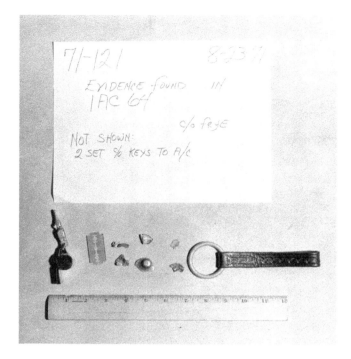

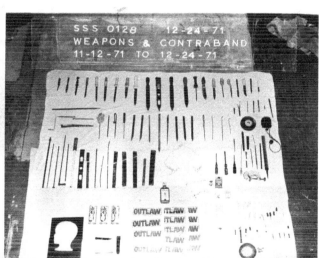

Even the smallest piece of a razor blade or other sharp object can be fashioned into a weapon by inmates with nothing but time on their hands and mayhem on their minds. In less than six weeks at the end of 1971, officers confiscated these potentially lethal weapons and other contraband in cell searches.

Dedicated, hard-working San Quentin Officers Frank DeLeon, Paul Krasenes, and Sergeant Jere Graham. End of Watch: August 21, 1971.

Almost immediately following George Jackson's bold escape attempt from the Adjustment Center, the Reagan Proclamation helped to make the working environment safer for officers and staff. One such change was adding a gated sallyport to the Lockup entrance, as these before and after photos show.

In 2012, I was honored to participate on a panel at a Corrections conference
with these heroes from two catastrophic prison riots just three weeks apart:
San Quentin, August 21, 1971, and Attica, September 9, 1971.
Left to right: San Quentin hostage survivor Officer Rubi Rubiaco;
Attica hostage survivor Officer Don Almeter; myself; and
Attica hostage survivor Officer John Stockholm.

WHERE ARE THEY NOW?

WARDEN LOUIS 'RED' NELSON stayed on as warden after the incident in the Lockup and eventually retired from San Quentin. Born on the Rosebud Indian Reservation in South Dakota, he became a deputy sheriff in Goldfield, Nevada, before beginning his Corrections career in California at Alcatraz. He worked his way up from correctional officer to warden in his twenty-six-year career. He retired as a warden at San Quentin, and stayed in Marin County, where we'd occasionally meet for lunch. He died in June 2001 at age 91.

WARDEN ROBERT A. HEINZE worked for the California Department of Corrections from 1917 to 1966. In 1927 he became a supervising parole officer at San Quentin, and was warden of Folsom State Prison for the last twenty-two years of his service. He is deceased.

CORRECTIONS DIRECTOR RAY PROCUNIER managed the California Department of Corrections from 1967 to 1975. Procunier also headed up the prison systems in Utah, Virginia, and New Mexico. In early 1984 he signed on as the director of the Corrections Department in Texas, but retired just thirteen months later, saying he had simply "run out of gas." Procunier passed away in January 2010 at the age of 86.

ASSOCIATE WARDEN JAMES PARK was the acting warden on Aug. 21, 1971. He left San Quentin shortly after the riot in the Lockup. He is deceased.

OFFICER DANIEL P. SCARBOROUGH was a Purple Heart recipient for battles fought in WWII and Vietnam. Scarborough retired from Corrections in 1979 after eleven years at San Quentin. He passed away in February 2016 in Pocatello, Idaho. He was 92.

LIEUTENANT MIKE LUXFORD transferred to another correctional facility several years after the riot, working as a correctional counselor II. He is deceased.

LIEUTENANT WILLIAM SELLMER suffered a heart attack a couple of years after the 1971 riot. He regained his health and finished his career in a position at the Richard A. McGee Correctional Training Center in Galt, California.

LIEUTENANT EUGENE ZIEMER was a submarine commander in the Navy before his career in Corrections. He left the profession a couple of years after the 1971 riot, choosing a life as a Colorado rancher instead. He passed away in 2008 at the age of 90.

LIEUTENANT AL STEWART resigned from the Department of Corrections shortly after the riot, and went to work for the Marin County Sheriff's Department, rising to the rank of lieutenant before he retired.

OFFICER WILLIAM TWELLS retired in 1981 after twenty-four years in the Department, but never faded far away from his brothers and sisters in Corrections, with whom he kept in contact until his death in January 2003.

CORRECTIONS EXPERT CARL LARSON began his career in 1960 as a correctional officer at San Quentin State Prison. Over the years, Larson promoted within the Department to sergeant, correctional supervisor II, lieutenant, captain, program administrator, correctional administrator, chief deputy warden, warden, and regional administrator. When he retired in 2012, he had served over half a century in Corrections. Larson passed away unexpectedly one morning in September 2013, as he prepared to lead a monthly meeting of the planning committee for a national Corrections museum in Sacramento.

OFFICER STEVE CAMBRA was working North Block on Aug. 21, 1971. Cambra served the California Department of Corrections as an officer, warden, and chief deputy director before retiring in 2001. He worked another eleven years as an annuitant in the Department's field medical operation. He is currently a member of the planning committee for a national Corrections museum in Sacramento.

◆

OFFICER CHAD BRECKENRIDGE left the Corrections profession shortly after the incident. His last known work was as a clinical social worker and college professor in Minnesota.

SERGEANT KEN McCRAY left Corrections work altogether sometime after the 1971 riot. He declined to discuss the August 21 riot with us, indicating he has no desire to revisit the incident.

OFFICER URBANO 'RUBI' RUBIACO transferred out of San Quentin shortly after the incident in 1971. It was determined to be too dangerous for him to be on the ground at San Quentin, so he was reassigned to another institution. Rubiaco went on to serve a long and distinguished career in Corrections. After receiving a degree from Sonoma State University, he promoted to parole agent and served another fifteen years in Corrections before his retirement. Rubi was a dedicated professional through and through. While being interviewed by special investigators at 10 p.m. in his home following the riot and a trip to the hospital,

Rubi told them, "I'll try to get back to work as soon as I can." He died in 2013 shortly after being interviewed for this book. He was 66.

GUNWALK/BALCONY OFFICERS Following the August 21, 1971, riot, the two officers who returned fire on the armed Jackson as he ran from the Lockup were relocated under protection orders. Each officer fired one round and one round only on that day, and each hit what he was aiming for.

◆

THE SAN QUENTIN SIX

FLEETA DRUMGO, along with Soledad Brother John Clutchette, was acquitted in 1972 of murder in the 1970 killing of Soledad Correctional Officer John Mills. In 1976, Drumgo was acquitted of all charges in the 1971 riot. He was released from prison in August 1976 but was shot to death in Oakland three years later.

DAVID JOHNSON, who was already serving a sentence of five years to life on a burglary conviction, was convicted of one count of assault for his part in the 1971 riot. He was released from prison in 1993.

HUGO 'YOGI' PINELL was convicted of two counts of felony assault by a prisoner serving a life sentence for his role in the 1971 incident. Habitual offender Pinell was serving six life sentences for various convictions – including a 1965 rape, the murder of Soledad Officer McCarthy in 1971, and his assaults on San Quentin Officers Breckenridge and Rubiaco in 1971 – when he was stabbed to death on a yard at California State Prison, Sacramento, in August 2015. He was killed just days after being released back into the general population.

JOHNNY SPAIN was the only one of the San Quentin Six convicted of conspiring with Jackson to murder officers. However, his conspiracy conviction in the riot case was later overturned on the grounds that the shackles he wore during the trial may have prejudiced the jury. He paroled in 1991.

LUIS TALAMANTEZ, who was serving time on a 1966 armed robbery conviction at the time of the San Quentin riot, was acquitted of all charges in the incident. He was released from prison in August 1976. In 1985, he was thought to be living somewhere in the south.

WILLIE TATE was acquitted of all charges in the 1971 incident, but wound up back in prison in later years on drug offenses. In the mid-1980s, he was reported to be a fugitive on a drug warrant in California.

◆

ANGELA DAVIS, once thought to be more than just a comrade to George Jackson, was a member of the Black Panthers, and an all-black branch of the Communist Party. Since the 1970s she's been advocating for women's rights, civil rights, and prison reform. She is currently a professor at the University of California, Santa Cruz.

STEPHEN BINGHAM, George Jackson's acting attorney on August 21, 1971, fled the country immediately following news of the riot. He lived in various places in Europe before returning in 1984 to surrender to charges of smuggling the weapon in to Jackson during a visit at the prison on the day of the riot. He was acquitted of murder and conspiracy in 1986. Following the trial, Bingham reportedly worked in legal aid offices and law firms in San Francisco and Oakland. His status with the State Bar of California became inactive in 2015.

VANITA ANDERSON, a legal investigator on George Jackson's legal team, was initially interviewed following the incident in 1971, but she declined to cooperate with state investigators. The FBI decided not to interview her regarding the incident. After the riot, she reportedly returned for a time to Texas, and in more recent years had been an instructor at Los Angeles Community College.

◆

JUDGE TERRENCE BOREN was the Marin County deputy district attorney in 1971, and the prosecuting attorney for the sixteen-month-long San Quentin Six trial. He was also assigned to prosecute the case against Stephen Bingham in 1985, a trial that lasted about six months. Boren later became a superior court judge in Marin County, and is currently active in the Assigned Judges Program in Northern California.

INVESTIGATIVE LIEUTENANTS GEORGE WATKINS AND PAUL DOBREFF Following the riot, Watkins continued his career at San Quentin as a correctional counselor II. When he passed away, his family asked that his memorial service be held in the prison chapel, and the warden approved that request. The chapel was packed wall-to-wall with convicts and staff. Dobreff worked in many capacities throughout his thirty-two years in Corrections, including at conservation camps, Soledad Prison, CRC, and San Quentin. He retired in 1985 as an associate warden at San Quentin. He is deceased.

GLOSSARY

ADJUSTMENT CENTER (AC)
Also known as the Lockup at San Quentin. The housing unit that houses the most dangerous inmates on the property. See also Lockup.

ADMINISTRATIVE SEGREGATION (Ad Seg)
The jail within the prison. It houses noncompliant inmates. See also Lockup.

ARMORY
The building where weapons and related defense equipment are stored.

BATON
A solid wood or plastic defense tool about eighteen inches long with a leather strap attached at one end; sometimes referred to as a billy club. See also Tear Gas Billy.

BGF
Black Guerilla Family, a prison gang of black inmates, founded by San Quentin inmate George Jackson in the late 1960s.

CDC / CDCR
The California Department of Corrections and Rehabilitation (formerly the California Department of Corrections) is the government agency tasked with operating the state's prison and parole systems.

CLASSIFICATION
The Corrections Department's system of assessing inmates' risk of misconduct potential to determine their housing security level (1, 2, 3, or 4) and degree of supervision while incarcerated. The assessment is based on several criteria, such as term length, gang membership, number of prior

incarcerations, and behavior exhibited during those prior incarcerations. Level 1 is considered minimum or low risk; Level 4 is maximum or high risk.

CLEAR the COUNT
Officers in housing units count the inmates at separate times during the day. They then must reconcile the number of inmates in their housing units with the control sergeant and the numbers on the Daily Movement Sheet in order to clear the count.

CONCERTINA WIRE
A type of coiled barbed wire that is attached to the top of prison boundary fencing meant to discourage escapes.

CONDEMNED ROW (or DEATH ROW)
Condemned Row refers to the cells housing the inmates who've been sentenced to death for their crimes. In California, three areas at San Quentin house male

condemned inmates: the East Block, North Segregation Unit, and the Adjustment Center. Female condemned inmates are housed at Central California Women's Facility in Chowchilla. At this writing, there is a moratorium on executions in California.

CONTRABAND
Illegal or prohibited items or substances, such as weapons or drugs, that are smuggled into a correctional facility.

CONTROL CORRIDOR
The foyer just inside the housing unit entrance.
DEATH ROW
See Condemned Row.

DMS
The Daily Movement Sheet that contains the record of all movement of inmates throughout the facility, including cell moves, arrivals, departures, and inmate job assignment changes.

FISH
A new officer; a rookie or newbie. Also an inmate who is new to prison.

GASSING
A type of assault that involves an inmate throwing collected bodily fluids on an officer or staff member, usually in the face.

GENERAL POPULATION
The group of inmates classified as those at little risk for trouble.

GRILL GATE
A floor-to-ceiling barred gate separating the tier of cells from the corridor or foyer of the housing unit.

HONOR BLOCK
The housing unit for inmates meeting a certain criteria based on good behavior.

INFORMANT
Also snitch or rat. An inmate who willingly shares information with officers or prison officials about assaults, potential violence, or planned uprisings.

INSPECTOSCOPE GATE
The metal-detecting device used to catch contraband items coming into the prison, such as small weapons or drugs secreted inside clothing or the body. All individuals coming onto the property must successfully pass through the metal detector or be denied entrance.

JOINT
Another word for prison. Max joint is a maximum security prison.

LOCKUP
Another name for a prison's Adjustment Center (AC), Administrative Segregation (Ad Seg), or Security Housing Unit (SHU) designed to house noncompliant or particularly dangerous inmates.

LWOP
A sentence of Life Without (the possibility of) Parole.

THE MAN
A law enforcement officer.

POST
A designated area or assignment that an officer works during his or her watch.

POTTY WATCH
The assignment of watching an inmate who is suspected of consuming contraband brought in from the outside. The inmate is placed in a special cell and is on continual watch until the suspected item is expelled through defecation, and retrieved and inspected by an officer.

PROGRAM
Refers to the behavior of inmates to follow the Department's rules of incarceration while serving their sentences.

PRUNO
Booze secretly made by inmates in their cells using fruit combined with a yeast product, such as bread or rolls, then left to develop into an alcoholic liquid.

QUIET CELL
A cell that has been stripped of everything, including the sink and toilet (there is a hole in the floor with a push button for flushing), so an unruly inmate cannot create noise and chaos on the tier. In addition, the mattress and all bedding are removed from the cell's bunk until nighttime. Inmates placed in quiet cells receive daily medical checks.

SALLY PORT
A secure, gated entryway into the prison property or to a building on the property, such as the Adjustment Center at San Quentin.

SCOOPING THE BRASS
Retrieving any spent cartridges left on the floor

after a weapon has been fired. This is to prevent an inmate from remanufacturing the empty cartridge into a live round of ammunition.

SECURITY HOUSING UNIT (SHU)
The jail within the prison for unruly or especially violent or dangerous inmates, such as the SHU at Pelican Bay State Prison near the Oregon border. See Lockup.

SHANK
An inmate-manufactured knife or stabbing weapon; also sometimes called a shiv.

SHIFT
See Watch.

TEAR GAS BILLY
A law enforcement baton, or billy club, that can also shoot a tear gas cartridge.

THE THOMPSON (aka Mr. Thompson)
An American sub-machine gun invented in 1918 by John T. Thompson; also known as a Tommy gun.

THROW THE BARS
To open a cell or a group of cells.

TIER
The 'floor' of cells within a cell block or housing unit.

TIER TENDER or TRUSTY
A mostly compliant prisoner who can be trusted to assist without incident with the daily operations of the prison through labor assignments such as office work, cleaning, and distributing meals.

WATCH (Shift)
California correctional facilities run security staff 24/7 on three eight-hour shifts: first watch, second watch, and third watch. Depending on the institution, first watch (night shift) is typically in the vicinity of 11 p.m. to 7 a.m., second watch (day shift) is 7 a.m. to 3 p.m., and third

watch (evening shift) is 3
p.m. to 11 p.m.

Additional prison jargon:

BACK DOOR PAROLE
To die in prison.

BONE YARD
The family visiting
apartments.

GREEN APPLE
The gas chamber at San
Quentin.

HARD TIME
Serving a long sentence.

JACKET
An inmate's reputation,
usually used in a derogatory
sense.

KEISTER
To conceal drugs, money, or
weapons in the rectum.

KITE
A note or letter illicitly sent
or received by an inmate.

MOOSE LIPS
Cold cut meats in a brown
paper bag lunch.

LIP
A lawyer or advocate.

THE OLD MAN
The prison warden.

ROAD DOG
An inmate's best friend.

UNCLE
Any federal law enforcement
officer.

THE WHITE HOUSE
The warden's residence at
San Quentin.

ZOOM ZOOMS and
WHAM WHAMS
Goodies from the prison
canteen or a package from
the streets.

REFERENCE NOTES

During the course of researching and writing this book, my collaborators and I thoroughly studied countless print and online newspaper articles, magazines, books, and other media on: Corrections in California; San Quentin, Folsom, and Attica prisons; George Jackson, the Soledad Brothers, and the San Quentin Six; and the many incidents that tie them all together – particularly the events of August 1971.

That research, together with my four decades working in the industry, the Department's five-hundred-page investigative report, and our conversations with individuals who played integral roles within the stories here all contributed to this memoir and the true crime story that embedded itself within the pages of my life.

News articles and opinion pieces were often buried deep within the archives of some news carriers whose long-held political leanings could not be ignored as a reflection of the social climate of the time. Some of the information we found in the many stories written or produced on the subject of the events of August and September 1971 that took place at San Quentin State Prison and Attica Correctional Facility is boldly presented as fact and truth, when we know it is anything but.

Those are their stories. This is mine.

Because this book is a narrative of a time in my life, no other type of reference will be quite as important or unique as my own experiences. Nothing ever written on these intense subjects by any journalist, historian, or storyteller will ever compare with the actual experiences of the men and women who lived through the events described in this book. Those will forever be our most fundamental and noteworthy pieces of research.

Print and online newspapers, magazines, videos, reports, and books we reviewed include:

- The Marin Independent Journal
- The San Francisco Chronicle
- The San Francisco Examiner
- East Bay Times (originally the Contra Costa Times)
- San Francisco Bay View
- The Los Angeles Times
- The New York Times
- The Sacramento Bee
- The Desert Sun, Palm Springs/Coachella Valley
- Santa Cruz Sentinel
- Oxnard Press-Courier
- The Day, New London, Conn.
- Newsweek
- USA Today
- KRON TV – *Day of the Gun: The George Jackson Story; 2002*
- Joint Legislative Committee Hearings on Prison Construction & Operations, 1983, California State Legislature
- CDC Departmental Incident Report, September 1971
- U.S. Department of Justice, National Institute of Corrections
- U.S. Department of Justice, Bureau of Justice Statistics
- odmp.org (Officer Down Memorial Page)
- cpof.org (Correctional Peace Officers Foundation)
- correctionsone.com (CorrectionsOne online community)
- cdcr.ca.gov (California Department of Corrections and Rehabilitation, formerly CDC)
- foundsf.org (History of San Francisco digital archive)
- history.com
- rollingstone.com

- wikipedia.org
- britannica.com
- *Behind San Quentin's Walls: The History of a Prison and its Prisoners* by William B. Secrest
- *Incident at San Quentin: How a Pistol Was Smuggled Into San Quentin* by Daniel P. Scarborough
- *Soledad Brother: The Prison Letters of George Jackson* by George Jackson
- *American Saturday* by Clark Howard
- *The Rise and Fall of California's Radical Prison Movement* by Eric Cummins
- *The Road to Hell: The True Story of George Jackson, Stephen Bingham, and the San Quentin Massacre* by Paul Liberatore
- *Blood in the Water: The Attica Prison Uprising of 1971 and its Legacy* by Heather Ann Thompson
- *Captive Nation: Black Prison Organizing in the Civil Rights Era* by Dan Berger

ACKNOWLEDGMENTS

The idea for this book began rather simply, as most books about prison riots *do not*, I imagine. I wanted to put together a memoir, mainly for my family history. I wanted my children and my children's children to know more about me, about Shirley, about our life together, and my long career in Corrections.

But this project soon took on a life of its own. As I started meeting regularly with my collaborators – my friend and longtime Corrections expert Don Novey, and fellow writer Patti Sewall – it was as if a snowball started to roll slowly downhill somewhere off in the distance. We couldn't grab it and stop the motion or change the direction. Nor did we want to.

It didn't take us long to see a greater significance in telling the story of a career spent in a uniform working behind the wall. Paragraph by paragraph, we began to recognize that telling this story now was important for today's correctional peace officers who wear the same uniform I did, carry the same title, work the same post, but in a different time and culture.

As we unraveled this almost unimaginable true crime story that happened nearly five decades ago, we began to understand another purpose beyond a simple memoir. We wanted the story to show the critical roles that intuition, responsibility, courage, and common sense play in protecting public safety.

Into Harm's Way is as much an homage to the people who mentored me along the way so many years ago as it is a gesture of friendly guidance to new officers just graduating from the Corrections Academy. I hope you feel as proud to wear that uniform as I was. Remember to watch your back – and those of your fellow officers.

In remembrance of those who've made the ultimate sacrifice in this job, and those who still carry the scars of battles fought for the greater mission, I offer enormous thanks to my fellow officers. They were there on the forgotten battlefield behind the wall, in San Quentin's Lockup, that fateful day in August 1971. I suspect this project was somewhat driven from above by coworkers no longer with us, who also wanted the story told. My brave brothers and sisters in Corrections, *Thank you* for your fight-or-die-trying spirit that saves lives every day.

To those who participated in making this book a reality, I thank you from the bottom of my heart: Rubi Rubiaco, Steve Cambra, B.J. Kennedy, Jim Brown, Carl Larson, Attica survivors Don Almeter and John Stockholm, and other fellow Corrections professionals who stopped by during the process to share their unique wisdom and memories. Your invaluable knowledge and memorable experiences in the profession reflect the honor and courage it takes to do that job. To the current and former San Quentin officers who came by to offer a handshake in respect, I am humbled and appreciative. Your support for me and this project won't be forgotten.

Finally, I am extremely grateful for the countless hours, immeasurable expertise, companionship, and support I received from Don Novey, Patti Sewall, Glenn Mueller, and the Correctional Peace Officers Foundation. I could not have asked for more complete dedication to this project.

ABOUT THE AUTHOR

Richard A. Nelson retired as an Associate Warden in 1998 after a distinguished career of nearly 40 years of dedication to public safety in California.

A partial list of the more than seventy professional acknowledgments Nelson received throughout his career:

- President, Marin County Peace Officers Association, 1992 - 1993.

- Letter of Appreciation from the director of the California Department of Corrections for contributing to the Task Force on the Commission of Felony Crimes; corroboration in writing three Felony Criminal Training manuals for correctional employees, 1988.

- Letters of Commendation from California Dep. Attorney General Bruce Slavin and the Department of Corrections for efforts in establishing the Security Housing Unit Law Library. The library was the first in California created exclusively for inmates in Lockup, and exceeded the standard established by the U.S. Circuit Court of Appeals for the Ninth District, 1987.

- Emergency Training Departmental Controller at five California correctional facilities, 1986 and 1987.

- Recognized for his professional assistance by Women in Corrections, a group dedicated to enhancing the promotional potential of women working in the department, 1980.

- Certificate of Professional Achievement, CDC, Conflict Resolution, 1978.

Nelson is the founder of the San Quentin Museum, and throughout his career he worked as a script consultant on numerous television and film productions shot in and around Folsom State Prison and San Quentin State Prison.

In 2012, he wrote the book *Waiting for George: Letters from the Shipyard*, a compilation of his father's letters home while working the West Coast defense industry shipyards during WWII.

Nelson now lives in Northern California where he keeps active with memberships in local sports, law enforcement, and museum associations and clubs, and sits on the steering committee for the National Big House Prison Museum project. He is a bona fide history buff and a fisherman at heart.

CPSIA information can be obtained
at www.ICGtesting.com
Printed in the USA
LVHW032039081019
633405LV00002BA/685/P